INDEX TO THE 1850 MORTALITY SCHEDULE OF SOUTH CAROLINA

BY

BRENT H. HOLCOMB, C.A.L.S.

Please Direct All Correspondence and Book Orders to:

Southern Historical Press, Inc.
PO Box 1267
375 West Broad Street
Greenville, SC 29602-1267
or
southernhistoricalpress@gmail.com

----

southernhistoricalpress.com

ISBN #0-89308-194-9

Printed in the United States of America

INTRODUCTION

The mortality schedule is one of the most valuable and least used portions of the U. S. census. It was taken along with the census each time from 1850 to 1880. Within this census is found the name of the deceased, age, sex, color, whether free or slave, marital status, place of birth (just as the regular census), death month, profession, disease or cause of death, and the number of days ill. The researcher should be aware that this is for persons who have died in the year previous to the taking of the census. The 1850 mortality schedule, indexed here, is the first one to show slaves by name and age, and is the only way to determine states of birth for many person (since previous census records did not show this). The sample page from the original shows best what the mortality schedule is like.

Unlike most Federal census records, the original return of the mortality schedule is housed in the South Carolina Archives. Specific pages may be order from them for a fee, or the entire 1850 mortality schedule may be purchased on microfilm for $15.00. Please keep in mind that this book is only an index to the original, and information like that on the sample page will be available on each deceased person.

A three letter abbreviation for each district has been used followed by the page number within that district on which the name occurs. Slaves names are inconsistent: some show only a first name, some show owners names, and some show both first and last names. The following are the abbreviations used for the districts:

ABB Abbeville
AND Anderson
BAR Barnwell
BEA Beaufort
CHA Charleston
CHR Chester
CFD Chesterfield
COL Colleton
DAR Darlington
EDG Edgefield
FAI Fairfield
GEO Georgetown

GRE	Greenville	ORA	Orangeburgh
HOR	Horry	PIC	Pickens
KER	Kershaw	RIC	Richland
LAN	Lancaster	SPA	Spartanburgh
LAU	Laurens	SUM	Sumter
LEX	Lexington	UNI	Union
MRN	Marion	WIL	Williamsburgh
MBO	Marlboro	YRK	York
NEW	Newberry		

My thanks to Mr. Allan Shull of Lexington, South Carolina, for his help in alphabetizing these names.

Brent H. Holcomb, C. A. L. S.
Box 21766
Columbia, S. C. 29221
February 10, 1980

SCHEDULE 3.—Persons who Died during the Year ending 1st June, 1850, in _______ **in the**

County of Greenville **State of** So Carolina **, enumerated by me,** H. T. Thompson **Ass't Marshal.**

	NAME OF EVERY PERSON WHO DIED during the Year ending 1st June, 1850, whose usual Place of Abode at the Time of his Death was in his Family.	DESCRIPTION. Age.	Sex.	Colour (White, black, or mulatto).	Free or Slave.	Married or widowed.	PLACE OF BIRTH. Naming the State, Territory, or Country.	The Month in which the Person died.	PROFESSION, OCCUPATION, OR TRADE.	DISEASE, OR CAUSE OF DEATH.	Number of DAYS Ill.
	1	2	3	4	5	6	7	8	9	10	11
1	Elizabeth Pence	66	F			M	Virginia	Sept		Apoplexy	[illegible]
2	Wm Coleman	1	M				So Ca	March		Teething	[illegible]
3	Malinda	30	F	B	S		So Ca	Aug		Dysentery	30 days
4	Infant	3/12	F	B	S		So Ca	Feb		do	2 days
5	Infant	3/12	F	B	S		So Ca	Aug		do	[illegible]
6	Leon	8	M	B	S		So Ca	July		do	30 days
7	William	10	M	B	S		So Ca	July		do	[illegible]
8	Infant	1/12	M				So Ca	Jan		Unknown	[illegible]
9	Thomas	11	M				So Ca	Sept		Unknown	[illegible]
10	Mary Hooker	41	F				So Ca	Feb		Consumption	[illegible]
11	Alex McMillen	16	M				So Ca	Sept	Laborer	Fever	12 days
12	Benjamin Turner	13	M				So Ca	April	Laborer	Fever	[illegible]
13	John	2	M	B	S		So Ca	April		Croup	[illegible]
14	[illegible]	[illegible]									

17	Sarah Moore	80	F			W	Virginia	July		Old age
18	Samuel Crane	13	M				So Ca	March		Unknown
19	Joseph Thompson	80	M			M	So Ca	April	Farmer	Old age
20	Will Ferguson	85	M			M	Virginia	Jan	Farmer	Dropsy
21	George	45	M	B	S		So Ca	June		Unknown
22	Susan Leister	28	F			M	So Ca	Jan		Cold
23	Mary	4/12	F	B	S		So Ca	Oct		Accident
24	Nancy Taylor	33	F			M	So Ca	Feb		[illegible]
25	Solomon Howell	3	M				So Ca	April		Worms
26	William Blakely	5	M				So Ca	May		Bronchitis
27	Infant	5/12	M	B	S		So Ca	Sept		Whooping c[illegible]
28	David Duncan	5/12	M				So Ca	Nov		Hives
29	John	18	M	B	S		So Ca	Oct		Fever
30	Clary James	80	F			W	Virginia	April		Dropsy
31	Jenny	65	F	B	S		Virginia	April		Fever
32	Pinckney Green	20	M				So Ca	Jan	Farmer	Fever
33	Permela	9/12	F	M	S		So Ca	April		Hives
34	Catherine Enslow	40	F			M	So Ca	June		Childbed
35	Jacob Enslow	1/12	M				So Ca	July	✓	[illegible]

Remarks:

Aaron, slave NEW 6
Aaron, slave NEW 10
Aaron, slave GEO 7
Aaron, slave of E. Jones ABB 2
Aaron, slave of E. Still EDG 7
Aaron, Wm BAR 4
Abbey, slave SUM 1
Abbey, slave of George Getzer EDG 15
Abbey, slave of Mary Maynad EDG 10
Abby, slave of L. Covin ABB 3
Abby, slave of C. Ruffs Est. ABB 15
Abednego, slave ORA 8
Abels, John L. AND 5
Abernathy, Martha NEW 9
Abiecrombia, Lewis, slave of LAU 8
Ables, Wane slave LEX 3
Abner, slave of Elizabeth BurressEDG 1
Abner, slave of Thomas Garrett EDG 1
Abner, slave of P. Rogers ABB 3
Abolem, slave of J. H. Hughes EDG 6
Abraham, slave GRE 5
Abraham, slave LAN 1
Abraham, slave RIC 2
Abraham, slave NEW 5
Abraham, slave of Willis AlsobrookCFD 3
Abraham, slave of Wm. P. Ingraham CHA 1
Abraham, slave of T. W. Porcher CHA 3
Abram, slave BEA 12
Abram, slave BAR 4
Abram, slave BAR 8
Abram, slave COL 4
Abram, slave GEO 8
Abram, slave of Simeon Matthews EDG 5
Abrams, Sarah M. LAU 5
Absolom, slave LAN 4
Absolem, slave SPA 3
Acker, M. slave of AND 4
Acker, P. M. slave of AND 4
Adaline, slave SUM 11
Adaline, slave SUM 12
Adaline, slave SUM 8
Adaline, slave SPA 4
Adaline, slave of John Barlow EDG 9
Adaline, slave of Josias Lanham EDG 16
Adaline, slave of H. M. Prince ABB 7
Adaline, slave of J. R. Wever EDG 3
Adam, slave NEW 8
Adam, slave ORA 7
Adam, slave FAI 7
Adam, slave BAR 3
Adam, slave BAR 9
Adam, slave CHA 12
Adam, slave SUM 9
Adam, slave SUM 7
Adam, slave SUM 12
Adam, slave of W. H. Davis ABB 18
Adam, slave of Dr. T. G. Prioleau CHA 1
Adam, slave of Capt. Robertson CHA 2
Adams, A. W. slave of EDG 11
Adams, Anna AND 5
Adams, Archy(?), slave of LAU 1
Adams, Charles slave RIC 1
Adams, Dick slave RIC 1
Adams, E. EDG 7
Adams, Elizabeth AND 5
Adams, H. LAN 4
Adams, H. H., slave of EDG 16
Adams, J. S. slaves of ABB 16
Adams, Jas. F., slave of EDG 11
Adams, John slave of EDG 1
Adams, Joseph, slaves of EDG 17
Adams, Joshua NEW 4
Adams, Kaziah, slave RIC 1
Adams, Maurice, slave RIC 1
Adams, Phoebe, slave RIC 1
Adams, Sam BAR 13
Adams, Tansey, slave RIC 1
Adar, slave of Jordan Holliway EDG 12
Addis, slave of Josiah Hinnant FAI 3
Addison, slave WIL 2
Addison, slave ORA 9
Addison, Allen B. EDG 11
Addison, Patience, family of EDG 11
Addison, T. A., slave of EDG 9
Addy, George, slave of EDG 19
Addy, Henry LEX 2
Adeline, slave GRE 6
Adeline, slave WIL 5
Adkins, D., slave of ABB 9
Aelene, slave YRK 3
Affa, slave SUM 10
Affay, slave COL 12
Affey, slave GEO 6
Affey, slave GEO 4
Affy, slave COL 8
Affy, slave of D. Peagler CHA 13
Agatha, slave of Alexander McQueenCFD 1
Aggy, slave SUM 11
Aggy, slave UNI 4
Aggy, slave UNI 7
Aggy, slave of S. R. Morrah ABB 3
Agnes, slave of M. Hutchinson ABB 18
Agnes, slave of J. M. Latimer Sr ABB 13
Agnes, slave of S. R. Morrah ABB 3
Agnew, S. W., slave of ABB 12
Agnus, slave CHA 12
Ahrens, C. CHA 17
Ahrens, ChristopherCHA 17
Aiken, Clarence C. FAI 6
Aiken, J. slave of ABB 7
Aiken, James, slave of FAI 1
Ailsey, slave NEW 2
Airs, Anthony CHA 25
Albert, slave YRK 2
Albert, slave MBO 1
Albert, slave of W. W. Walling EDG 2
Albert, R. KER 4
Alewine, Barbara LEX 3
Alewine, Sena NEW 7
Alex, slave ORA 8
Alex, slave BAR 7
Alexander, slave NEW 7
Alexander, slave NEW 4
Alexander, slave YRK 3
Alexander, slave SPA 1
Alexander, A. DAR 2
Alexander, Ansalem PIC 6
Alexander, Charity UNI 7
Alexander, David AND 1
Alexander, ElizabethSUM 6
Alexander, Jack, slave PIC 4
Alexander, L. LAN 4
Alexander, Nancy SPA 1
Alexander, Nancy PIC 4
Alexander, Sarah A KER 4
Aley, slave NEW 6
Alford, slave SUM 1
Alford, Daniel HOR 1
Alford, Noah HOR 2
Alfred, slave SUM 9
Alfred, slave GRE 1
Alfred, slave GRE 6
Alfred, slave MRN 2
Alfred, slave ORA 2
Alfred, slave of J. A. Mars ABB 4
Alfred, slave of Sarah Pace ABB 12
Alguire, John ABB 12
Alguire, Robert ABB 12
Alice, slave of G. McDuffie ABB 13
Alick, slave MRN 3
Alison, Sarah, Slave of LAU 7
All, Ann COL 2
All, Margret LEX 2
Allen, slave NEW 6
Allen, slave of J. P. Graves ABB 3
Allen, slave of Keran Hearn EDG 17
Allen, slave of Thomas McKie EDG 15
Allen, slave of J. Riley ABB 9
Allen, slave of D. Ruff ABB 19
Allen, Catherine BAR 6
Allen, Charles BAR 10
Allen, Emmelina (free black) CHA 27
Allen, Fanny slave CHA 22
Allen, J. T., slave of ABB 13
Allen, J. V., slave of ABB 6
Allen, John C., family of EDG 6
Allen, Mary SPA 1

Allen, William CHA 19
Allen, Zachariah HOR 1
Allison, Hugh YRK 5
Allston, J. slaves of ABB 6
Allon, slave of T. P. Lipscombe ABB 18
Alma, slave of F. W. Pickens EDG 9
Almond, Amanda MRN 2
Alonzo, slave UNI 6
Alsobrook, Willis, slaves of CFD 3
Alston, William, slaves of FAI 4
Altman, James WIL 4
Alzina, slave BAR 2
Amanda, slave BAR 9
Amanda, slave NEW 4
Amanda, slave of S. B. Brooks ABB 11
Amanda, slave of James Harper FAI 8
Amanda, slave of N. Hughey ABB 9
Amanda, slave of L. C. Jeter UNI 2
Amanda, slave of L. A. Latimer ABB 14
Amber, slave FAI 1
Ambers, slave of __ Mobley FAI 1
Ambler, James PIC 4
Ambrose, slave SPA 3
Ame, slave COL 11
Amelia, slave BEA 12
Amelia, slave LAN 5
Amelia, slave GRE 1
Amelia, slave COL 1
Amelia, slave of J. Floyd ABB 18
Amelia, slave of Dr. Gaillard CHA 1
Amelia, slave of S. Lee ABB 4
Amey, slave SUM 12
Amey, slave ORA 8
Amey, slave DAR 2
Amey, slave SUM 4
Amey, slave of John B. Holmes EDG 6
Amey, slave of Shade Holmes EDG 1
Amick, George A. LEX 2
Amick, George A., slave LEX 2
Amos, slave NEW 4
Amos, slave COL 11
Amos, slave LAN 3
Amos, slave UNI 5
Amos, slave of S. McClellan CHA 9
Amy, slave MBO 3
Amy, slave COL 1
Amy, slave GEO 4
Amy, slave FAI 8
Amy, slave BAR 10
Amy, slave of M. L. Bonham EDG 11
Amy, slave of Z.Harris EDG 13
Amy, slave of Charlotte LambethCFD 1
Anaca, slave of Sarah LaBrode EDG 8
Anacy, slave of Jonothan Tayler EDG 15
Ancrum, C. D. KER 3
Ancrum, T. J., slaves of KER 5
Anderson, slave FAI 4
Anderson, slave NEW 7
Anderson, slave of R. M. Davis ABB 14
Anderson, slave of S. W. NicholsonEDG 6
Anderson, David HOR 2
Anderson, Edith E. HOR 2
Anderson, George D., slave of EDG 2
Anderson, J. S., slave of ABB 13
Anderson, James Al.EDG 15
Anderson, Joel S., slave of LAU 6
Anderson, John CHA 19
Anderson, Mrs. GEO 9
Anderson, Mary BAR 7
Anderson, Robert ABB 17
Anderson, Robert EDG 15
Anderson, Samuel NEW 9
Anderson, Sarah, slave PIC 1
Anderson, Thomas M., slave EDG 2
Anderson, William. slave of LAU 3
Andrew, slave BAR 8
Andrew, slave of W. Lesly ABB 7
Andrew, slave NEW 6
Andrew, slave MBO 3
Andrew, slave ORA 4
Andrew, slave of Benj. Boulware FAI 8
Andrew, slave of Poppenheim CHA 12
Andrew, slave of S. A. Tillman EDG 6
Andrews, Allen LAU 2
Andrews, Ephraim, slave of EDG 10
Andrews, Wm., slave of EDG 7
Andrial, Priscilla SUM 4
Andy, slave FAI 3
Andy, slave UNI 5
Andy, slave GRE 8
Andy, slave of D. L. Wardlaw ABB 6
Aney, slave DAR 1
Angeline, slave WIL 5
Angelina, slave of F. OConnor EDG 6
Anhoney, slave GEO 7
Ann, slave DAR 2
Ann, slave YRK 2
Ann, slave BAR 2
Ann, slave UNI 8
Ann, slave LAN 1
Ann, slave LAN 2
Ann, slave MRN 2
Ann, slave MRN 1
Ann, slave ORA 3
Ann, slave NEW 8
Ann, slave NEW 3
Ann, slave NEW 6
Ann, slave of M. Burkhalter EDG 8
Ann, slave of F. W. Calliham EDG 16
Ann, slave of Archey Clark EDG 10
Ann, slave of A. T. Drafton EDG 15
Ann, slave of D. Lesly ABB 6
Ann, slave of A. Miles EDG 18
Ann, slave of T. Moore ABB 17
Ann, slave of L. J. Patterson ABB 2
Ann, slave of J. A. Stevenson UNI 2
Ann, slave of Posey Trussel AND 1
Ann, slave of William J. Wight-manEDG 17
Anna, slave BAR 13
Anna, slave BAR 7
Annetta, slave WIL 2
Annette, slave of Dr. Gaillard CHA 1
Annette, slave of ABB 7 A. Martin
Annis, slave of J. H. Hughes EDG 6
Annis, slave of J. McCartney Est ABB 2
Annis, slave of J. Watsons Est. ABB 10
Anny, slave WIL 3
Anny, slave ORA 3
Anny, slave of W. Sartor UNI 1
Ansel, slave COL 12
Anslem, slave COL 3
Ansley, Jesse ABB 5
Anson, slave ORA 1
Anson, slave of William Walker EDG 15
Anson, Ann T. CHA 21
Anthony, slave ORA 8
Anthony, slave SUM 14
Anthony, slave SUM 5
Anthony, slave SUM 10
Anthony, slave SUM 14
Anthony, slave of J. M. Carson ABB 9
Anthony, slave of George McKie EDG 15
Anthony, slave of Dr. J. P. Scriven BEA 2
Antley, Cathrine ORA 9
Antoinette, slave of D. R. Sartor UNI 1
Antonia, slave COL 12
Antony, slave MRN 3
Apollo, slave BAR 9
Ara, slave ORA 2
Arch, slave of Rebecca Simpson PIC 6
Archer, A. H. SPA 3
Archer, John P. PIC 2
Archy, slave of O. Towles EDG 7
Ard, Anne MRN 1
Armsted, slave of Samuel Clarke EDG 2
Armstrong, James, slave of AND 1
Armstrong, Lantina ABB 5
Armstrong, Margaret CHA 22
Arnold, Bonetta CHA 25
Arnold, Mary E. PIC 2
Arrants, M. A. KER 4
Arthur, slave of W. Templeton ABB 17

Arthur, Cynthia BAR 10
Arthur, Henry LEX 4
Arthur, Henry, slavLEX 4
Ashcraft, Mary L. YRK 1
Asheford, Gilbert LFAI 2
Ashmore, Ann GRE 3
Ashmore, James GRE 6
Ashmore, Maria GRE 3
Assmann, Maryan LEX 4
Assyria, slave GEO 3
Ataway, David EDG 4
Ataway, James, slave of EDG 4
Atchison, Eugene EDG 4
Atkinson, Jonah GEO 9
Auba, slave of K. Simmes Sr. CHA 1
August, slave COL 3
August, slave COL 8
August, slave COL 12
August, slave SUM 1
Augusta, slave of EDG 1 Tandy Burkhalter
Augustin, slave GEO 8
Augustus, slave NEW 4
Aull, Caroline E. NEW 9
Ausker, slave WIL 4
Austin, slave NEW 10
Austin, slave NEW 4
Austin, slave of CFD 1 Ellerbe B. C. Cash
Austin, Alexandria LAU 4
Austin, Henry J. LAU 4
Austin, Jane GRE 2
Austin, Robert GRE 2
Austin, Robert, slave of LAU 1
Axon, John Est. CHA 10
Austin, Rosa GRE 6
Autry, Hails GRE 3
Autry, Luke GRE 3
Autry, Matilda GRE 3
Avinger, Catharine ORA 3

Babe, slave UNI 6
Babit, slave of M. C. Tallman ABB 4
Bachman, Lucy, slave CHA 26
Bacot, R. H. slavesBEA 15
Bailey, Alexr slaveKER 1
Bailey, Ann COL 7
Bailey, Ann E. SUM 9
Bailey, B. LAN 5
Bailey, F. Julia GEO 5
Bailey, Henry, slave of LAU 1
Bailey, J. W. AND 7
Bailey, James BAR 8
Bailey, John D. LAU 1
Bailey, Jonas C., slave of LAU 7
Bailey, Mary COL 11
Bailey, Mary BAR 14
Bailey, Rachel BAR 14
Bailey, S. E. AND 7
Bailey, Sofrona LAU 4
Bailey, Unise BAR 14
Bailey, Wade, slaveKER 1
Bailey, William CHA 6
Baily, Salina MRN 3
Baily, Richard COL 2
Bain, Jas GRE 1
Bain, Mary GRE 3
Baker, Aaron SUM 5
Baker, James WIL 1
Baker, John W. CFD 1
Baker, Lindsey, slave of AND 9
Baker, William, slaves LEX 4
Baker, William F. NEW 9
Ball, J. C., slaves of CHA 2
Ball, Keating, slaves of CHA 2
Ball, W. J., slaves of CHA 7
Ball, William C. ABB 12
Ballard, John EDG 4
Ballard, M., slaveKER 4
Ballenger, Joel SPA 1
Bane, infant UNI 4
Bangy, slave GEO 5
Bankhead, John G. UNI 5
Banks, Bryant ABB 2
Banks, Martha, slave PIC 1
Banks, S., slave of FAI 3
Banks, Samuel ABB 2
Barbara, slave of EDG 14 Iverson J. Brock
Barbary, slave of Z. Harris EDG 13
Barber, Anna ORA 3
Barber, George YRK 5
Barber, Jas H CHR 1
Barber, Jane CHR 1
Barefield, George KER 2
Barger, infant NEW 2
Barger, J. C. NEW 2
Barker, Dr. S. W., slaves of CHA 1
Barkley, J. T. LAN 2
Barksdale, S., slave of ABB 2
Barksdale, Samuel, slave of LAU 3
Barksdale, W., slave of ABB 13
Barlay, slave SPA 3
Barlow(?), John, slave of EDG 9
Barmore, William ABB 12
Barnes, T. LAN 4
Barnes, Z. V., slave of ABB 5
Barnet, Dolly A. AND 7
Barnet, J. J., slave of ABB 7
Barney, slave NEW 10
Barns, Elizabeth ABB 6
Barnwell, Affy, slave BEA 8
Barnwell, Margaret BEA 10
Barnwell, May, slave BEA 8
Barnwell, Nelly, slave BEA 8
Barnwell, Toby BEA 8
Barnwell, Will BEA 8
Barny, slave BAR 13
Barpany, slave of Jordan Holliway EDG 12
Barre, John P. NEW 9
Barre, Noah M. NEW 10
Barret, D. SPA 3
Barret, James A., slave YRK 5
Barrett, Earl H. PIC 4
Barrett, Massey G. SUM 13
Barrot, J. P., slave of ABB 10
Barrot, J. P., slave of ABB 10
Barter, Thomas EDG 14
Bartlet, slave NEW 3
Bartlett, Ann E. SUM 3
Barton, Dorcas PIC 2
Barton, Shaply GRE 1
Barwic, Stephen ABB 1
Bash, slave BEA 12
Bashee, Martha BEA 10
Bates, Martha BAR 5
Bates, Mary, slave RIC 1
Bates, Thos S., slave of EDG 18
Bathias, slave MRN 3
Bauchman, Christian CHA 26
Baughman, Abram BAR 9
Baughnight, Elias, slave LEX 3
Baughnight, Mary LEX 2
Bauskett, J., family of EDG 5
Bauskett, John, family of EDG 5
Baynard, Judy, slave BEA 9
Baynard, Minty, slave BEA 9
Baynard(?), Rich BEA 10
Bazer, David BAR 1
Beam, Laura A. NEW 5
Bean, Elizabeth CHR 4
Beard, Rebecca ABB 19
Bearden, John ABB 4
Bearegard, SusannaYRK 5
Beasley, Bessy C., slave LAU 4
Beatrice, slave of E. Jones ABB 2
Beatty, Ruth A. AND 9
Beatty, Waller YRK 5
Beauford, infant UNI 8
Beaufort, Francis, slave KER 4
Becca, slave GEO 2
Beck, slave SUM 7
Beck, slave of B. Huger ABB 8
Beck, slave of H. C. Miller PIC 2
Beck, Caroline BAR 5
Beck, Caroline BAR 9
Beckey, slave of D. C. Moore ABB 16
Beckham, Jacob, slave RIC 3
Beckham, M. LAN 3
Beckham, W. F. LAN 3
Beckham, William LAN 5
Beco, Sarah Jane AND 2
Bedenbaugh, Mat-thias H. EDG 19
Bedenbaugh, MichaelNEW 6
Bee, B. E., slave of AND 6
Bee, Maria AND 6
Beggy, slave COL 12
Belcher, B. E., slave of ABB 4
Belew, Jane UNI 4
Belew, William UNI 4
Beley, slave WIL 2
Belk, M. H. L. LAN 3
Bell, child BAR 9
Bell, slaves of FAI 2

Bell, Elizabeth CHR 1
Bell, George, slave of EDG 18
Bell, J. E. G., slave of ABB 13
Bell, James., slaves of LAU 6
Bell, John HOR 2
Bell, John CHR 1
Bell, Joshua EDG 1
Bell, Mary E. LAU 7
Bell, Wm., infant slave CHA 12
Bella, slave SUM 10
Bella, slave BEA 12
Bella, slave ORA 9
Bella, slave of Mr. Colburn CHA 9
Bella, slave of W. P. Ingraham CHA 7
Bella, slave of W. P. Ingraham CHA 8
Bella, slave of Thos H. Murree CHA 1
Bella, slave of Susan A. Roper EDG 16
Bellee, slave COL 3
Bellflowers, Theodore MRN 1
Bellflowers, Thomas MRN 1
Bellon, slave NEW 2
Bellotte, Jacob, slave of AND 7
Belton, slave NEW 6
Bembo, slave COL 11
Ben, slave ORA 8
Ben, slave ORA 9
Ben, slave BEA 13
Ben, slave WIL 2
Ben, slave COL 4
Ben, slave WIL 4
Ben, slave WIL 3
Ben, slave BAR 3
Ben, slave SUM 8
Ben, slave SUM 6
Ben, slave UNI 5
Ben, slave SUM 13
Ben, slave of H. H. Criswell ABB 17
Ben, slave of A. Harris ABB 4
Ben, slave of J. Holland ABB 19
Ben, slave of F. L. Kay ABB 15
Ben, slave of R. Laurens CHA 7
Ben, slave of G. McDuffie ABB 13
Ben, slave of T. P. Mosely ABB 16
Ben, slave of J. S. Partlow ABB 11
Ben, slave of John W. Rochell EDG 17
Ben, slave of Joseph Shanklin PIC 5
Benford, slave NEW 6
Bengo, Amelia CHA 15
Bengo, Hermina CHA 15
Benj., slave of G. O. Wilkinson EDG 14
Benjamin, slave NEW 9
Benjamin, slave NEW 9
Benjamin, slave of Wm. Andrews EDG 7
Benjamin, slave of J. G. Lamar EDG 14
Bennet, Frances CHA 16
Bennet, Mary BAR 9
Bennet, Virginia CHA 23
Bennett, Thos., slaves of CHA 2
Benny, slave FAI 3
Benson, slaveof J. Smith ABB 16
Benson, E. B., slave of AND 8
Benson, Prew GRE 5
Benton, Rachel COL 1
Bernard, Francis CHA 19
Bernice, slave NEW 6
Berry, slave BAR 7
Berry, slave of William Donn(?) EDG 4
Berry, Ann M. ORA 6
Berry, Mary YRK 1
Berry, Mary CHA 26
Berry, Thos EDG 20
Bess, slave WIL 4
Bess, slave GEO 1
Bess, slave of Mrs. M. Bonneau CHA 13
Bess, slave of W. Dunn ABB 12
Bess, slave of N. B. Henning CHA 6
Bess, slave of G. C. Jemey CHA 6
Bessellen, Charles BEA 11
Best, Absalom BAR 14
Betsey, slave BAR 1
Betsey, slave CHA 5
Betsey, slaveof J. S. Anderson ABB 13
Betsey, slave of Alexander Walker EDG 17
Betsey, slave of J. Wideman ABB 4
Betsy, slave WIL 5
Betsy, slave SUM 14
Betsy, slave SUM 6
Bettey, slave YRK 2
Bettis, Benja., slave of EDG 3
Bettis, Lucy, slave of EDG 16
Betts, Francis CHA 16
Betts, Virginia CHA 27
Betty, slave FAI 2
Betty, slave FAI 2
Betty, slave ORA 1
Betty, slave BEA 11
Betty, slave COL 9
Betty, slave COL 3
Betty, slave GEO 6
Betty, slave MRN 3
Betty, slave MBO 2
Betty, slave BAR 9
Betty, slave CHA 10
Betty, slave SUM 4
Betty, slave SUM 12
Betty, slave LAN 1
Betty, slave of Saml Clarke EDG 2
Betty, slave of J. H. Guerrard BEA 2
Betty, slave of S. Lee ABB 4
Betty, slave of W. Morrison ABB 15
Betty, slave of T. P. Mosely ABB 16
Betty, slave of S. S. Palmer CHA 9
Beverly, slave of J. Watson ABB 10
Bickley, John J. NEW 4
Bigby, G., slave of ABB 14
Bigger, Amos YRK 5
Bigham, Elizabeth CHR 2
Bigham, Octavius MRN 1
Bill, slave HOR 1
Bill, slave WIL 5
Bill, slave YRK 4
Bill, slave YRK 2
Bill, slave BAR 10
Bill, slave CHA 12
Bill, slave SUM 7
Bill, slave of Ellerbe B. C. Cash CHF 1
Bill, slave of Chas Foster CHA 3
Bill, slave of Jas Ownesby EDG 13
Billa, slave COL 11
Billet, slave of Tilmon Watson
Billingslie, Catharine MBO 4
Billy, slave COL 3
Billy, slave COL 12
Billy, slave DAR 1
Billy, slave ORA 4
Billy, slave SUM 11
Billy, slave SUM 13
Billy, slave of J. L. Allen ABB 6
Billy, slave of J. C. Ball CHA 2
Billy, slave of Keating Ball CHA 2
Billy, slave of Revd. D. Dupree CHA 11
Billy, slave of J. Harleston CHA 7
Billy, slave of Allen McFarland CFD 1
Billy, slave of WM. Whelden CHA 6
Binah, slave BAR 11
Bina, slave MRN 1
Binah, slave COL 1
Binah, slave WIL 4
Binah, slave RIC 2
Binah, slave COL 12
Binah, slave SUM 13
Binah, slave of Wm. P. Ingraham CHA 1
Bing, Almond BEA 13
Bing, Matilda BEA 13
Bing, Rebecca BEA 13
Binky, slave GEO 8
Binky, slave SUM 7
Binn, slave of Charlott Prior EDG 2
Bird, Eldred slave of EDG 12
Bird, Susan E. WIL 5
Bird, T. B., slave of ABB 11
Bivens, Francis ABB 3
Black, Mike, slave RIC 3
Black, Nancy H., slave LAU 4
Black, Oliver LAU 7
Black, Susey RIC 3
Black, Tompey, slave RIC 3

Black, W., slaves of ABB 7
Black, Washington ABB 14
Black, Wm. BAR 13
Black, William YRK 5
Blackaby, B., slave of ABB 19
Blackburn, John LAU 5
Blackmon, A. LAN 4
Blackmon, G. LAN 3
Blackwell, Isaah EDG 13
Blackwell, James, family of EDG 11
Blair, Mary FAI 2
Blair, Thomas FAI 2
Blake, slave COL 9
Blake, A., slaves of CHA 10
Blake, John ABB 11
Blake, Joicy EDG 14
Blake, Walter, slaves of BEA 3
Blakely, William GRE 4
Blakeney, John, slave of CFD 3
Blalock, Wosela(?), slave of EDG 9
Bland, Luke EDG 1
Blane, William CHA 17
Blanam(?), John KER 3
Blassingam, R., slave of AND 2
Bledsoe, Abigal EDG 12
Boatoman, slave GEO 4
Boatright, George LEX 3
Boatswain, slave of Saml Reid PIC 5
Bob, slave COL 10
Bob, slave COL 8
Bob, slave COL 9
Bob, slave COL 1
Bob, slave ORA 3
Bob, slave ORA 9
Bob, slave YRK 1
Bob, slave DAR 3
Bob, slave DAR 3
Bob, slave BAR 5
Bob, slave SUM 9
Bob, slave SUM 12
Bob, slave of J. B. Adamson ABB 1
Bob, slave of Thomas M. Anderson EDG 2
Bob, slave of J. C. Ball CHA 2
Bob, slave of Benja. Bettis EDG 3
Bob, slave of E. R. Calhoun ABB 11
Bob, slave of J. N. Cochran ABB 15
Bob, slave of J. Floyd ABB 18
Bob, slave of J. S. Gibbs CHA 6
Bob, slave of L. Griffin ABB 15
Bob, slave of Thomas W. Harbin PIC 5
Bob, slave of Milly Harris ABB 4
Bob, slave of B. Huger ABB 8
Bob, slave of W. Lesly ABB 7
Bob, slave of J. A. Mars ABB 4
Bob, slave of S. Reid ABB 15
Bob, slave of R. Sproull ABB 18
Bob, slaveof Stanmore Watson EDG 18
Bockelhoff, H. L. CHA 17
Bockelhoff, Peter C. CHA 17
Boddy, Joel LEX 3
Bodie, J. P., slave of EDG 18
Boland, Abraham M NEW 10
Boland, Magdaline NEW 10
Boland, Reuben T. NEW 10
Bolar, slave of Atticus Tucker EDG 4
Bold, Mary BEA 10
Bolding, Wm PIC 4
Bolin, Bretton YRK 5
Bolt, Abraham LAU 8
Bolt, Harriet C. LAU 8
Bolt, Wade LAU 8
Bolware, H., family of EDG 5
Bone, Catharine GEO 1
Bone, H. Thos MBO 3
Boneau, John E. CHA 24
Bonest, Robert, slave CHA 22
Bonham, M. L., slave of EDG 11
Bonneau, Ann E. CHA 25
Bonneau, Mrs. M., slave of CHA 13
Bonner,Ann SPA 1
Bonnet, Judah BAR 6
Bonnet, Sally BAR 6
Bonnet, Wash BAR 6
Booney, Jacob LEX 1
Beoth, Lafayette EDG 3
Boozer, Catherin, slave LEX 3
Boozer, David LEX 3
Boozer, David NEW 2
Boozer, Lucinda NEW 4
Boozer, Nancy NEW 4
Boss, slave of S. T. Fourdin CHA 13
Boston, slave BAR 4
Boston, slave BAR 11
Boston, slave ORA 4
Boston, slave MBO 4
Boston, slave of A. Harris ABB 18
Bouknight, Wm., slaves of EDG 19
Boulware, Benj., slave of FAI 8
Boulware, M., slave of FAI 1
Boulware, Martha FAI 5
Boulware, Robert LAU 1
Bourman, James COL 1
Bouthron, Francis CHA 19
Bow, slave of Perry Holliway EDG 4
Bowen, Ailsey KER 1
Bowen, William, slave of LAU 9
Bowen, Woody ABB 7
Bowers, J. W. NEW 1
Bowers, Julia BAR 12
Bowers, Martha EDG 2
Bowker, S., slaves of UNI 2
Bowman, Mary BAR 6
Bowie, Handy, slave CHA 19
Boyd, Amelia A. YRK 1
Boyd, Eleanor WIL 5
Boyd, John A. ABB 7
Boyd, Lemuel C. NEW 4
Boyd, Mary Ann WIL 5
Boyd, Rachel YRK 1
Boyd, Samuel A., slave of LAU 3
Boyd, Sarah T. WIL 5
Boyed, Daniel A. HOR 3
Boykin, C. C. KER 4
Boykin, Solomon, slave KER 4
Boylston, Elijah BAR 6
Boylston, George BAR 6
Braddock, John CFD 2
Bradford, Rebecca M. SUM 13
Bradford, Robt SUM 13
Bradham, Henry SUM 4
Bradley, Mary GRE 5
Bradley, Sarah PIC 4
Bradshaw, Henry WIL 1
Brady, Edward CHA 18
Brady, R., slaves of ABB 3
Brady, Thomas ORA 8
Brady, Thomas JunORA 8
Brailsford, Robin, slave CHA 24
Brakefield, Elizabeth CHR 5
Bram, slave COL 1
Bramlet, Jno GRE 6
Bramlet, Thomas GRE 2
Brandy, slave of Dr. William C. Daniels BEA 1
Brass, slave GEO 8
Brass, slave of A. Mazyck CHA 11
Brass, slave of R. McBride FAI 6
Bratham, Francis BAR 12
Brazeal, Griffin AND 2
Brazil, M. LAN 4
Breazeal, Eugenia AND 3
Breazeal, Kennon, slaves of AND 3
Brezeal, W., slave of AND 2
Bredenberg, Diederich CHA 26
Breeden, J. AND 1
Breland, Thos BAR 1
Breland, Thos BAR 14
Bremer, William (free mulatto) CHA 22
Brevard, Ann, slave RIC 1
Brevard, H. C., slaves of KER 5
Brevard, Isabel, slave RIC 1
Brevard, Mary, slave RIC 1
Brevard, Milly, slave RIC 1
Brevard, Priscilla, slave RIC 1
Brevard, Rillah, slave RIC 1
Brewer, Hannah K. AND 4
Brewer, Martha J. AND 3
Brewer, Tabbitha AND 3
Brian, John R. O. PIC 6

Briant, Caroline AND 3
Briant, James AND 3
Briant, Permelia AND 3
Briant, Simon, slave of AND 4
Brice, J., slave of FAI 3
Brice, J. C., slave of FAI 1
Brice, S., slave of FAI 3
Brice, Saml SPA 3
Brice, Walter, slave of FAI 3
Bridges, Wm MBO 1
Briggs, infant BAR 2
Briggs, Orlando UNI 5
Brigheyes, slave GEO 1
Brissey, William GRE 8
Brister, slave SUM 2
Brister, slave GEO 4
Brister, slave of D. Gent ABB 14
Britt, Mary, slaves of ABB 1
Broadie, Wm. BAR 14
Broadwater, Yarborough, slave of EDG 16
Brock, female child AND 1
Brock, Iverson J., slaves of EDG 14
Brock, James AND 1
Brocklebank, Wm. CHA 18
Brogan, William CHA 18
Brogdon, Mary A. SUM 1
Brooker, Mary BEA 12
Brooks, Hester MRN 1
Brooks, Jane, slave of EDG 19
Brooks, Littleton A., slave of EDG 17
Brooks, M---, slave of LAU 8
Brooks, Maria M. NEW 5
Brooks, P. S., slave of EDG 16
Brooks, P. S., slaves of ABB 8
Brooks, S. B., slaves of ABB 11
Brooks, W. B., slaves of ABB 11
Brooks, W. P., slaves of ABB 10
Broom(?), Robert YRK 5
Brown, infant UNI 4
Brown, Beedy SUM 13
Brown, Danl, slave of AND 6
Brown, Eliza CHA 16
Brown, Elizabeth L BAR 2
Brown, J. L. CHR 1
Brown, John CHA 21
Brown, John, slaves of KER 1
Brown, John J. LAU 7
Brown, Jno LAN 4
Brown, Larkin G. YRK 1
Brown, Margaret HOR 1
Brown, Mary AND 8
Brown, Mary B. CHA 20
Brown, Nelly slave KER 1
Brown, Wm., slave of EDG 13
Brown, William WIL 3
Brown, William G. CHA 16
Brown, Weltha HOR 1
Brown, Winney UNI 6
Browning, Richard UNI 7
Brownlee, J., slaves of ABB 8
Brownlee, William ABB 8
Bruce, John, slave of AND 8
Bruerton, Susanna GEO 5
Brumby, Thos M. SUM 4
Brunson, D. D., slave of EDG 17
Brunson, John BAR 14
Brunson, Nelson, slave of BEA 14
Brunson, Sarah SUM 4
Bruton, Elizabeth HOR 1
Bruton, Thomas N. EDG 13
Brutus, slave SUM 9
Bryant, slave of John Everett EDG 2
Bryant, Mary GRE 6
Bryant, Sarah SUM 3
Bryson, John, slave of LAU 4
Bston, slave of Revd. D. Dupree CHA 11
Buchanan, Nancy, slave CFD 2
Buchanan, Robert ABB 19
Buchanan, RobertC ABB 19
Buck, slave of Rebecca Sartor UNI 1
Buckhalter, infant BAR 10
Buckhalter, M., slave of EDG 8
Buckner, Benjamin F, slaves of BEA 2
Buff, slave GEO 7
Buffkin, H. F. GEO 5
Bull, E. B. CHA 18
Bull, J. B., slave of ABB 2
Bull, Margaret ORA 3
Bunch, William UNI 6
Bungy, slave COL 2
Burdette, William, slave LAU 5
Burdin, James NEW 7
Burdine, Abram PIC 1
Burdine, Davis PIC 1
Burdine, Jane PIC 1
Burgess, Andrew SUM 2
Burgess, Elizabeth CHA 9
Burgess, James A. WIL 1
Burgess, Joshua GRE 5
Burket, Thomas, slave LEX 1
Burkhalter, Randy, slaves of EDG 1
Burnett, Matilda EDG 8
Burnett, Nancy ABB 18
Burns, Eli M. EDG 19
Burnside, Hanah, slave of LAU 3
Burrell, slave LAN 2
Burress, Elizabeth, slaves of EDG 1
Burris, E., slave of AND 8
Burris, Thomas AND 5
Burrows, Emma L. WIL 4
Burt, Dr. W. N., family of EDG 11
Burton, James NEW 3
Bush, Mary, slave of EDG 3
Bussee, Ann, slave of EDG 1
Butcher, slave COL 12
Butler, Cuffy, slave BEA 9
Butler, George W. ABB 9
Butler, Henry EDG 8
Butler, John A., slave of EDG 15
Butler, Levi SUM 4
Butler, M. J. NEW 3
Butler, Mary, slave of EDG 2
Butler, Patrick CHA 28
Butler, Starren MRN 3
Butler, Timothy, slave BEA 9
Bryant, Sarah BAR 14
Bynum, William RIC 1
Byrd, Elizabeth, slave of LAU 6
Byrum, J., child of AND 8
Bush, John BAR 7
Bythewood, Susan, slave BEA 9

Caesar, slave COL 4
Caesar, slave of Dr. William C. Daniels BEA 1
Caesar, slave of W. Thomas FAI 8
Cabe(?), slave GRE 7
Cain, slave SUM 3
Cain, slave COL 5
Cain, Anna M. SUM 5
Cain, James BAR 4
Cain, Martha ABB 18
Cain, S. V., slave of ABB 18
Cairey, Nancy YRK 3
Caity, slave COL 12
Calder, Violet G. CHA 21
Caldwell, slave UNI 8
Caldwell, David R. PIC 6
Caldwell, Isaac ABB 15
Caldwell, James J. RIC 3
Caldwell, Jane ABB 13
Caldwell, William H ABB 13
Caleb, slave ORA 9
Caleb, slave COL 2
Caleb, slave GEO 2
Calhoun, Aleck, slave PIC 1
Calhoun, Amanda C. ABB 19
Calhoun, D., slave of ABB 19
Calhoun, E., slave of ABB 3
Calhoun, E. R., slaves of ABB 11
Calhoun, Elizabeth, slave PIC 1
Calhoun, J. A., slaves of ABB 5
Calhoun, J. C., slave of ABB 13
Calhoun, Jim, slave PIC 4
Calhoun, John, slave PIC 1
Calhoun, John C. PIC 1
Calhoun, N., slave of ABB 19
Calhoun, P. L., slave of LAU 2
Calhoun, Sophia, slave PIC 1
Calhoun, W. C., slave of ABB 19

Calliham, F. W., slave of EDG 16
Callus, slave GEO 8
Calmes, F. F., slaves of LAU 5
Calvin, slave NEW 1
Calvin, slave of Natt Ellis BEA 2
Cameron, Abraham, slave CHA 23
Cameron, Jane CHA 19
Cameron, Matilda CHA 23
Camilla, slave SUM 13
Campbell, A. C., slave of AND 7
Campbell, Alex, son of AND 7
Campbell, Dido, slave BEA 9
Campbell, Duncan CFD 1
Campbell, Edward MRN 3
Campbell, Elizab. CHA 17
Campbell, Jane MRN 2
Campbell, Jesse MRN 2
Campbell, Mary MRN 2
Campbell, Mary ABB 8
Campbell, Mary P CFD 3
Campbell, Morgan MRN 2
Campbell, Plat, slave BEA 9
Campbell, W., slave of ABB 12
Camron, Zadock GRE 2
Candis, slave WIL 4
Candis, slave WIL 3
Candis, slave of Jordan Holliway EDG 12
Cannady, John CHA 22
Cannady, Margaret CHA 22
Cannon(?), John SPA 4
Cannon, M., slave of ABB 2
Cannon, Martha NEW 1
Cannon, Samuel NEW 9
Canought, Dennis CHA 16
Cantrell, F. J. SPA 4
Cantrell, Lawson SPA 4
Canty, A., slave KER 5
Canty, F., slave KER 5
Canty, J., slave KER 5
Capehart, J., slaves of EDG 10
Capers, Abner, slave BEA 7
Capers, Kitty, slave BEA 7
Capers, Rosana, slave CHA 16
Caple, Augustus S. SUM 9
Caradine, Elizabeth PIC 5
Carew, Edward CHA 25
Carew, J. E., slave of CHA 12
Carey, Caroline CHA 15
Carla, slave SPA 3
Carlisle, Charner UNI 7
Carlston, Magnus CHA 24
Carmon, Ann Eliza CHA 26
Carnes, Lewis, slave of EDG 2
Carolina, slave COL 4
Carolina, slave BAR 12
Carolina, slave BAR 13
Carolina, slave GRE 2
Carolina, slave of J. Martin ABB 8
Carolina, slave of S. W. Palmer CHA 13
Carolina, slave of Russel Vaughan EDG 9
Carolina, slave of J. R. Wever EDG 3
Caroline, slave YRK 1
Caroline, slave FAI 7
Caroline, slave MBO 2
Caroline, slave MRN 1
Caroline, slave GEO 6
Caroline, slave COL 1
Caroline, slave COL 5
Caroline, slave BAR 13
Caroline, slave SUM 12
Caroline, slave GRE 7
Caroline, slave GRE 6
Caroline, slave GRE 5
Caroline, slave GRE 5
Caroline, slave UNI 8
Caroline, slave AND 3
Caroline, slave of Dr. S. W. Barker CHA 1
Caroline, slave of R. Blassingam AND 2
Caroline, slave of Littleton A. Brooks EDG 17
Caroline, slave of E. Gains ABB 11
Caroline, slave of E. Lott EDG 18
Caroline, slave of Rebecca Love AND 3
Caroline, slave of E. Owen ABB 5
Caroline, slave of W. Means ABB 7
Caroline, slave of J. B. Richey ABB 15
Caroline, slave of G. Sibert ABB 1
Caroline, slave of W. Smith ABB 9
Carroll, Delilah BAR 5
Carroll, Thomas, slave YRK 5
Carroll, Wiley EDG 13
Carsen, Charles EDG 18
Carson(?), John SPA 4
Carson, J. M., slave of ABB 9
Carson, Wm. A., slaves of CHA 1
Carter, slave HOR 1
Carter, slave NEW 8
Carter, slave of Richard Griffin EDG 7
Carter, Charles B EDG 14
Carter, E., slave of ABB 16
Carter, J. DAR 2
Carter, John S., slave of EDG 7
Carter, Mahala COL 2
Carter, Pinckney SUM 1
Carter, Sarah MRN 1
Carter, Wm., slave of EDG 7
Carter, William AND 6
Carter, William H WIL 3
Carter, William S WIL 2
Cartlege, Margaret, slave of EDG 16
Caruths, L., slave of AND 7
Carver, Lewis PIC 2
Carwiles, Z. W., slave of EDG 7
Cary, slave of A. Vance ABB 11
Casey, William LAU 8
Cash, Ellerbe B. C., slaves of CFD 1
Cason, J., slave of FAI 1
Cason, Martha FAI 1
Cassman, Charlotte, slave CHA 15
Castle, George W. PIC 3
Caswell, slave BAR 9
Cate, slave SUM 11
Cate, slave GEO 8
Cates, Robert EDG 2
Catharine, slave SUM 2
Catharine, slave UNI 5
Catharine, slave of B. Jordan ABB 9
Catharine, slave of J. Logan ABB 9
Catharine, slave of William Prescott EDG 16
Catharine, slave of J. P. Robinson FAI 1
Catherine, slave COL 12
Catherine, slave GRE 2
Catherine, slave of R. Laurens CHA 7
Cathrine, slave ORA 7
Cato, slave BEA 13
Cato, slave NEW 10
Cato, slave of Mr. Villeponteaux CHA 4
Catoe, Mary SUM 9
Caty, slave SUM 11
Caty, slave GEO 2
Caty, slave GEO 4
Caty, slave GEO 8
Caty, slave SUM 3
Caty, slave of S. Jerman CHA 9
Caty, slave of Wm. E. Porcher CHA 2
Caty, slave of Dr. T. G. Prioleau CHA 1
Caughman, Hilliard, slave LEX 3
Caulder, James MBO 3
Cause, Walter, slave CHA 17
Cauthen, M. LAN 4
Cealy, slave COL 9
Ceasar, slave WIL 1
Ceasar, slave BAR 4
Ceasar, slave SUM 9
Ceasar, slave ORA 9
Ceaser, slave of Lucy Bettis EDG 16
Ceasar, slave of F. OConnor EDG 6
Celia, slave MBO 4
Celia, slave COL 2
Celia, slave UNI 4
Celia, slave UNI 8
Celia, slave NEW 5
Celia, slave of Ann Bussee EDG 1
Celia, slave of Z. Ellerbe CFD 2
Celia, slave of Elizabeth Gibson EDG 19
Cely, Obedience GRE 5
Cesar, slave BAR 12
Cesar, slave ORA 6

Cesar, slave of
J. P. Deveaux CHA 12
Ceurence(?), Hugh,
free black YRK 5
Chamberlan, E. H.,
slaves of EDG 1
Chamberlain, Thomas,
slave of EDG 13
Chambers, Julia BAR 10
Chamblee, Moses,
slaves of AND 2
Chance, slave of
Keating Ball CHA 2
Chancy, slave GRE 2
Chandler, Arnl J. SUM 13
Chandler, William EDG 12
Chaney, slave of
H. C. Turner EDG 5
Chaney, V. E. LAN 1
Chany, slave BAR 5
Chany, slave of
W. H. Gains ABB 11
Chany, slave of
A. Hunter ABB 8
Chany, slave of
E. Noble ABB 6
Chapam, John B. CHA 16
Chaplin, Abby,
slave BEA 6
Chaplin, Abner,
slave BEA 8
Chaplin, Alpin,
slave BEA 7
Chaplin, Amey,
slave BEA 8
Chaplin, Cudjoe,
slave BEA 7
Chaplin, H., estate,
slaves of BEA 15
Chaplin, Jacob,
slave BEA 6
Chaplin, James,
slave BEA 8
Chaplin, John,
slave BEA 8
Chaplin, Martin,
slave BEA 6
Chaplin, Mary,
slave BEA 6
Chaplin, Plato,
slave BEA 7
Chaplin, Reedy,
slave BEA 7
Chaplin, Renty,
slave BEA 7
Chaplin, Richard,
slave BEA 7
Chaplin, Sally,
slave BEA 7
Chaplin, Silvey,
slave BEA 7
Chapman, Gilbert M FAI 5
Chapman, John NEW 2
Chapman, John PIC 4
Chapman, John,
slave LEX 2
Chapman, Milly,
slave of CFD 1
Chapman, Nancy PIC 4
Chapman, Sarah E. FAI 5
Chappell, Hanna B LAU 1
Chappel, S. H.,
slave of FAI 4
Chappill, William LEX 4
Charity, slave ORA 9
Charity, slave COL 5
Charity, slave WIL 5
Charity, slave of
Jane Turner EDG 9
Charles, slave BAR 11
Charles, slave BAR 12
Charles, slave SUM 11
Charles, slave UNI 5
Charles, slave of
A. W. Adams EDG 11
Charles, slave HOR 1
Charles, slave GEO 1
Charles, slave COL 3
Charles, slave COL 10
Charles, slave YRK 1
Charles, slave DAR 4
Charles, slave NEW 10
Charles, slave ORA 2
Charles, slave NEW 9
Charles, slave NEW 8
Charles, slave FAI 3
Charles, slave ORA 1
Charles, slave ORA 4
Charles, slave ORA 3
Charles, slave ORA 6
Charles, slave FAI 7
Charles, slave of EDG 19
slave of Wm. Bouknight
Charles, slave of
P. S. Brooks EDG 16
Charles, slave of
William Cose AND 1
Charles, slave of
J. Dorn EDG 7
Charles, slave of
T. F. Croft EDG 3
Charles, slave of
G. Graves ABB 13
Charles, slave of
A. Griffin ABB 17
Charles, slave of
A. Hunter ABB 8
Charles, slave of
T. Jackson ABB 6
Charles, slave of
Thos Sally EDG 11
Charles, slave of
M. Smith ABB 16
Charles, slave of
John Tompkins EDG 17
Charley, slave BAR 12
Charley, slave of Dr.
Palmer CHA 3
Charlott, slave WIL 5
Charlott, slave WIL 3
Charlotte, slave GEO 5
Charlotte, slave COL 10
Charlotte, slave CHA 5
Charlotte, slave BAR 7
Charlotte, slave BAR 13
Charlotte, slave CHA 10
Charlotte, slave LAN 1
Charlotte, slave LAN 2
Charlotte, slave LAN 4
Charlotte, slave UNI 3
Charlotte, slave UNI 6
Charlotte, slave SUM 3
Charlotte, slave SUM 7
Charlotte, slave SUM 10
Charlotte, slave YRK 2
Charlotte, slave BEA 12
Charlotte, slave of
S. W. Agnew ABB 12
Charlotte, slave ofBEA 1
Washington Goettee
Charlotte, slave of
William Hendrick CFD 3
Charlotte, slave of
Robt D Killin CFD 1
Charlotte, slave
of D. Rudd ABB 19
Charlotte, slave EDG 16
of Elizabeth Samuel
Charlotte, slave
of F. Scaife UNI 1
Charlotte, slave
of W. Tennant ABB 3
Chatham, slave NEW 6
Chatham, T.,
slaves of ABB 11
Chavas, Levicy SUM 4
Cheatham, B. M.,
slaves of ABB 12
Cheatham, Benjamin
F. ABB 7
Cheatham, Sophia JABB 12
Cheek, Ellis LAU 7
Chesny, Thomas SPA 2
Chester, slave GRE 3
Chester, slave of
Mewco Samuel(?) EDG 16
Chevis, Langdon,
slaves of BEA 2
Childs, William ABB 6
Childs, Jane E.,
slave of ABB 1
Chiles, J. M.,
slave of ABB 1
Chiles, Lewis A ABB 1
China, slave UNI 8
Chipley, J. S.,
slaves of EDG 9
Chisolm, Edwd.
Estate, slaves of BEA 14
Chisolm, James J.,
slave BEA 14
Chisolm, Robert,
slave BEA 14
Chitty, Darley BAR 13
Chloe, slave BAR 11
Chloe, slave WIL 1
Chloe, slave COL 9
Chloe, slave of
J. McCully FAI 1
Chloe, slave of
W. Berry EDG 7
Chloe, slave of
J. E. Carew CHA 12
Chloe, slave of
John Maxwell PIC 5
Christian, slave ORA 9
Christianna, slave BEA 12
Choats, Rachel YRK 1
Christianna, slave SPA 1
Christopher, slave
of P. S. Brooks ABB 8
Christopher, William
ABB 13
Cicely, slave of
John S. Carter EDG 7
Cicero, slave COL 12
Cicero, slave of
J. T. Moore ABB 6
Cid(?), slave GRE 7
Cillo, slave WIL 5
Cilly, slave COL 9
Cinda, slave of
Thos K. Robeson CFD 1
Clacy, William CHA 23
Claig--see also Clay
Claig, Letitia EDG 7
Clanton, Jane KER 4
Clara, slave WIL 2
Clara, slave FAI 7
Clara, slave WIL 1
Clara, slave BEA 12

Clara, slave of R. C. Sharp ABB 12
Clarasy, slave GEO 6
Clarasy, slave SUM 8
Clardy, Charles W AND 3
Clardy, James, slave of LAU 7
Clardy, John, slave of AND 3
Clarenda, slave COL 10
Clarinda, slave COL 7
Clarinda, slave MRN 2
Clarisa, slave BEA 12
Clarisa, slave MRN 1
Clarisa, slave of Sally Miles EDG 3
Clarissa, slave GRE 5
Clarissa, slave GRE 2
Clarissa, slave MRN 3
Clark, Ann HOR 1
Clark, Archey, slave of EDG 10
Clark, Cinthia FAI 6
Clark, Cupid, slave RIC 3
Clark, Dolly, slave RIC 3
Clark, H., slave of ABB 18
Clark, H. H., slave of FAI 5
Clark, J. M. CHR 2
Clark, John CHA 18
Clark, John CHA 12
Clark, John M., slave of EDG 1
Clark, Kinion MBO 3
Clark, M. B., slaves of ABB 13
Clark, Mary MRN 2
Clark, Mary MBO 3
Clark, Simon, slave MBO 3
Clark, Solomon CHA 25
Clarke, Ann H. EDG 2
Clarke, Archy, slave of EDG 4
Clarke, Samuel, slaves of EDG 2
Clarke, Thomas UNI 6
Clarkson, Charles RIC 2
Clarkson, Daucus, slave RIC 2
Clarkson, Edward, slave RIC 2
Clarkson, Frances, slave RIC 1
Clarkson, Grace, slave RIC 2
Clarkson, Lucretia, slave RIC 2
Clarkson, Maria, slave RIC 2
Clarkson, Rhoda RIC 2
Clarkson, Rufus, slave RIC 2
Clarrissa, slave NEW 10
Clary Ann, slave ABB 12
Clary, James GRE 4
Clary, M. W., slaves of EDG 4
Claxton, Mary EDG 3
Claxton, Thomas, slave of EDG 3
Clawson, Jacob YRK 1
Clay,Agner EDG 6
Clay, James GRE 1
Clay, Moses S. ABB 4
Clay, Siney EDG 6
Clay, W. H., family of EDG 6
Clayton, Infants(?) BAR 11
Clayton, Sarah BAR 11
Clayton, Wm. BAR 11
Cleckley, P. F., slave of ABB 8
Clement, slave COL 3
Clement, Guy, slave CHA 25
Clement, Isabella CHA 25
Clement, Joseph, slave CHA 25
Clement, Matilda Ann AND 1
Clement, W. H., slave of AND 1
Clemons, A. DAR 1
Clemons, C. DAR 3
Cleveland, Rebecca (free mulatto) CHA 26
Clinkskale, J. B., slave of ABB 12
Cloa, slave of J. Gregory UNI 1
Cloay, slave DAR 1
Cloe, slave GEO 6
Cloe, slave ORA 6
Cloe, slave of F. W. Pickens EDG 8
Clytus, slave COL 7
Coate, Thomas K. NEW 2
Coats, Maryann YRK 3
Cobb, Edmund ABB 10
Cobb, J. W., slave of ABB 15
Cobbs, Maholda ABB 6
Cobbs, Phillip W. ABB 6
Cobb, Robert PIC 6
Cobra, Saml M. SUM 3
Cochran, Augustus BAR 7
Cochran, J., slave of ABB 15
Cochran, J. N., slave of ABB 15
Cochran, L., slave of EDG 17
Cochran, Rebecca BAR 5
Cockrel, Benjamin, slaves of FAI 1
Cockrel, J., slave of FAI 3
Coe, slave SUM 5
Coffa, G. LAN 1
Coffa, S. LAN 1
Cofee, Susan EDG 1
Cofee, Virginia EDG 1
Coffin, Thos, slaveBEA 7
Coffin, Allan, slave BEA 7
Coffin, David, slave BEA 7
Coffin, Philip, slave BEA 6
Coffin, Phillip, slave BEA 6
Coffin, Saml, slave BEA 6
Coffin, Thos, slave BEA 7
Cohen, Amy (mulatto)BAR 14
Cohen, Barney, (mulatto) BAR 14
Cohen, Isabella CHA 15
Cohen, Leopold CHA 21
Cohill, John CHA 21
Cohill, Mary CHA 21
Coker, Ann A. SUM 11
Colbum, Silvia, slave CHA 24
Colburn, slaves ofCHA 9
Colcock, Mary W. CHA 20
Colcock, R. W. CHA 20
Cole, Ann BEA 10
Cole, Daniel SUM 2
Cole, Fuleelma BEA 12
Cole, John, slave CHA 26
Coleman, slave BAR 9
Coleman, slave of S. G. Gowan ABB 3
Coleman, Abagail GRE 5
Coleman, Alsey, slave LAU 6
Coleman, Albert EDG 10
Coleman, Andrew J.LEX 3
Coleman, Benjr., slave of EDG 16
Coleman, D. R., slave of FAI 3
Coleman, J. R., slave of FAI 3
Coleman, James CHA 27
Coleman, Jas. A. EDG 8
Coleman, John, slave of EDG 19
Coleman, R. W., slaves of FAI 3
Coleman, Robert EDG 10
Coleman, Sarah EDG 17
Coleman, Wm GRE 4
Coleman, William, slave of EDG 19
Collier, Elias E. KER 4
Colliers, E., Est., slave of ABB 1
Collins, Caroline CHA 23
Collins, Dennis CHA 17
Collins, Dennis CHA 23
Collins, Edward CHA 22
Collins, George BAR 13
Collins, Mary SPA 3
Colson,John COL 2
Colvert, W. F. LAN 1
Comfort, slave GRE 2
Comodore, slave COL 8
Conard, slave of M. Hutchinson ABB 18
Conaway, slave of B. M. Cheatham ABB 12
Conn, Isabella ABB 8
Conner, Jerusha (free mulatto) ABB 16
Conner, Mourning (free black) ABB 16
Conners, Elizabeth P. LAU 5
Connoly, John CHA 27
Conyers, slave SUM 10
Coody, slave GEO 1
Coogler--see Googler
Cook, Alexander WIL 2
Cook, M. LAN 3
Cook, Mary, slave of LAU 9
Cook, Mary M. WIL 2
Cook, Tom, slave CHA 25
Cooker, Pemala E. LAU 7
Coole, William UNI 4
Cooly, Charlotte SPA 4
Coon, Betsey, slave RIC 3

Coon, Enoch J. NEW 8
Coon, George NEW 8
Cooper, slave GRE 5
Cooper, ElizabethHOR 3
Cooper, ElizabethHOR 1
Cooper, J. W., slave of EDG 7
Cooper, Lancy DAR 4
Cooper, Mary ABB 3
Cooper, MazeareanHOR 1
Cooper, Polly ABB 3
Cooper, Reubin, slave of EDG 8
Cooper, Wm ORA 2
Cope, Elizabeth BEA 14
Cope, Laura BEA 14
Copeland, John YRK 5
Cora, slave ORA 2
Corbit, Jane, slave CHA 20
Corby, Nelly, slave CHA 15
Corley, Arcadia EDG 12
Corley, Atticus EDG 13
Corly, Barbara, slave LEX 1
Corley, Daniel EDG 12
Corly, Lemuel A LEX 1
Corley, Lizner EDG 13
Corley, Thomas EDG 10
Cornchain, Joseph, slave of EDG 3
Cornelia, slave UNI 7
Cornelia, slave GEO 2
Cornelias, slave of E. Nelson ABB 2
Cornelius, slave COL 8
Cornelius, slave COL 4
Cose, Cooley AND 2
Cose, Francis AND 4
Cose, Joel, slaves of AND 1
Cose, William, slaves of AND 1
Cothran, J., slave of ABB 1
Cotton, Francis MEDG 3
Cotton, Mary EDG 3
Couner, A. P., slaves of ABB 5
Couner, T. A., slaves of ABB 16
Counts, David, slave LEX 2
Counts, J. H., slave of FAI 4
Counts, John H., slaves of LEX 2
Cousar, H. L. CHR 2
Cousart, M. J. LAN 3
Couturier, Mrs. Peter CHA 4
Couturier, Mrs. R. J., slave of CHA 13
Cover, John, family of EDG 11
Covin,E., slave of ABB 3
Covin, L., slave of ABB 3
Cowan, S. G., slave of ABB 3
Cox, A. M., slave of ABB 2
Cox, Clement EDG 2
Cox, Rody PIC 2
Coyburn, Mary NEW 9
Craig, M. LAN 3
Craig, Thos LAU 4
Crane, Samuel GRE 4
Crapps, Rachael BEA 1
Craps, Barbara LEX 3
Crawley, WilliamE CFD 3
Crawley, Mary C. CFD 3
Crayton, B. D., slave of AND 8
Creed, Mary ORA 4
Creemer, Emily AND 2
Creighton, Martha KER 2
Creps, John EDG 3
Cresa, slave of Moses Chamblee AND 2
Cresa (free mulat-to) AND 1
Cresiwell, George ABB 1
Cressey, slave SUM 1
Cresswell, Wm. S., slaves of AND 6
Crips, Lether CHA 12
Criswell, Ann ABB 2
Criswell, H. H., slaves of ABB 17
Critis, slave BEA 13
Critty, slave NEW 2
Crocker, C. SPA 4
Crofts, T. G., slave of EDG 3
Crogan, Dennis CHA 20
Crogan, Margaret CHA 21
Cromer, George B. ABB 9
Cromer, G. W., slave of ABB 9
Crook, Ann C. ORA 3
Croomer, A. E. NEW 7
Croomer, Martha NEW 8
Croomer, Nancy NEW 7
Crosby, Lucy, slaves of FAI 5
Crosby, Rebecca COL 2
Crosland, Mary MBO 2
Cross, Mary L. D. CHA 15
Croswell, John A. SUM 4
Croswell, R. DAR 3
Crouch, Lewis, slave of EDG 19
Crout, Dellila LEX 3
Crout, John LEX 3
Crovat, Tillion CHA 25
Cudjo, slave BAR 7
Cudjo, slave COL 10
Cudjo, slave of A. Huger CHA 7
Cudjo, slave of Shirley Whatley EDG 7
Cuffy, slave GEO 2
Cuffy, slave GEO 1
Cuffy, slave of Wm. A. Carson CHA 1
Cuffy, slave of T. Petigru ABB 17
Culbreath, Mary K.EDG 10
Culbreath, William, slave of EDG 10
Cumbo, slave of T. C. Haskill ABB 17
Cumming, Elizabeth ABB 1
Cummings, Mary COL 5
Cunningham, Holley LAU 7
Cunningham, J., Est., slaves of KER 2
Cunningham, Joseph KER 5
Cunningham, L., child of AND 6
Cunningham, Robert, slaves of LAU 4
Cupid, slave GEO 5
Currey, Mary J., (free black) YRK 5
Currie, Elizabeth MRN 1
Curtis, slave of W.Black ABB 7
Cuthbert, James, slaves of BEA 15
Culclazier, Wm., slave of EDG 3
Culler, Ann ORA 6
Cunningham, Alice S. EDG 2
Curenton,Abner GRE 3
Cuthbert, Sarah BEA 13
Cyrus, slave YRK 3
Cyrus, slave WIL 3
Cyrus, slave BEA 6
Cyrus, slave of Thos S. Murree CHA 1

Dacus, John A., slave of AND 3
Dacus, William GRE 3
Daer, slave of Wm. Garrett EDG 15
Daffney, slave DAR 4
Dafney, slave SUM 10
Dagnall, William EDG 1
Dale, Edwin C. ABB 5
Dallas, slave BAR 3
Dalsneth(??), Ann KER 3
Dalwig, Edward CHA 25
Dalzel, Joseph BAR 14
Dan, slave DAR 4
Dan, slave SPA 2
Dan, slave of Sarah Hammond EDG 15
Dandridge, Susan H COL 1
Dandy, slave SUM 9
Dangerfield, John, slave of CHA 1
Daniel, slave LAN 1
Daniel, slave MBO 1
Daniel, slave FAI 3
Daniel, slave NEW 1
Daniel, slave CHA 12
Daniel, slave BAR 6
Daniel, slave SUM 5
Daniel, slave SUM 10
Daniel, slave SUM 6
Daniel, slave of H. H. Adams EDG 16
Daniel, slave of S. Bowker UNI 2
Daniel, slave of C. C. Dubose CHA 13
Daniel, slave of Edwd D. Jerman CHA 9
Daniel, slave of Artemas Lewis EDG 16
Daniel, slave of F. W. Pickens EDG 8
Daniel, slave of C. Smith ABB 16
Daniel, slave of A. Tool CHA 9
Daniel, Wm., slave of EDG 18
Daniels, Dr. William C., slaves of BEA 1
Danl, slave COL 5
Danl, slave of John F. MiddletonEDG 15

Danner, Agnes, slave BEA 6
Danner, Ann BEA 13
Danner, Mary, slave BEA 6
Danner, N. J. BEA 10
Danner, Sarah, slave BEA 6
Dantzler, Lewis M CHA 12
Daphna, slave of C. Peterson EDG 7
Daphne, slave WIL 3
Daphne, slave of Wm Ducass CHA 9
Daphne, slave of Wm. P. Ingraham CHA 1
Daphne, slave of T. W. Porcher CHA 3
Daphney, slave GEO 3
Daphny, slave of J. Watson ABB 10
Darby, John CHR 5
Darcus, slave YRK 4
Darcus, slave NEW 2
Darcus, slave NEW 5
Darcus, slave NEW 3
Darcus, slave of Samuel Clarke EDG 2
Daricote, Rebecca ABB 4
Darnel, Susan PIC 5
Darnold, Wm. PIC 2
Darymple, Jane FAI 6
Daublin, slave of John Stingmaker EDG 14
Dave, slave UNI 6
Dave, slave MBO 3
Dave, slave BAR 5
Dave, slave BAR 7
Dave, slave of E. Pratt ABB 14
Dave, slave of Rebecca Simpson PIC 6
Dave, slave of Tilmon Watson EDG 18
Davenport, Martha GRE 3
Davenport, Matilda NEW 3
Davenport, William CHA 18
David, slave LAN 3
David, slave YRK 2
David, slave COL 12
David, slave WIL 4
David, slave MRN 2
David, slave WIL 1
David, slave NEW 8
David, slave ORA 8
David, slave NEW 1
David, slave BEA 11
David, slave SUM 9
David, slave of Minor Gladden FAI 1
David, slave of R. W. Hay ABB 7
David, slave of H. C. Hurlong EDG 2
David, slave of Wm. P. Ingraham CHA 1
David, slave of C. Smith ABB 16
David, slave of W. A. Williams AND 2
David, Peter WIL 4
Davids, Washington J. CHA 17
Davie, Col. F. W. CHR 3
Davis, A. G. MRN 1
Davis, Andrew PIC 5
Davis, C. F., slaveBEA 14
Davis, Elizabeth ENEW 5
Davis, Eurial(?) LAU 2
Davis, Harriet A ABB 6
Davis, Henry D SUM 1
Davis, Hester A ABB 14
Davis, James ABB 2
Davis, James EDG 12
Davis, John, slave of BEA 14
Davis, John B., slave of LAU 7
Davis, John W. WIL 4
Davis, Mariam CHA 21
Davis, Mary C. CFD 2
Davis, N. J., slave of ABB 5
Davis, Ned, slave CHA 24
Davis, R. M., slave of ABB 14
Davis, Robt SUM 4
Davis, Sarah FAI 5
Davis, Susan A ABB 1
Davis, W. H., slave of ABB 18
Davis, William CFD 2
Davison, David AND 2
Davy, slave BAR 3
Davy, slave of Miss H. Gaillard CHA 3
Davy, slave of J. Link ABB 5
Dawkins, slaves ofFAI 4
Day, Christopher CHA 18
Day, Louisa N. PIC 2
Day, Thomas ABB 18
Days, Julius, family of EDG 5
Dean, Edward GRE 1
Dean, Mary LAU 4
Deane, Thos, slave of AND 5
Deas, Alexander CFD 3
Deas, Dr. E. H., slave of CHA 3
Deas, Susan CHA 20
Deason, Mary J. ABB 2
Deavenport, Thos LAU 6
Debose, Ann BAR 10
December, slave of S. Deveaux CHA 13
Deen, Joseph, slaves of LAU 5
Deen, Washington EDG 7
Degan, John CHA 23
Dehay, Theodore UNI 8
Delanay, Mary CHA 27
Delaney, R. LAN 1
Delaughter, Nancy, slave of EDG 15
Delehan, Patrick CHA 23
Delia, slave GEO 8
Delia, slave RIC 2
Delia, slave COL 2
Delia, slave SUM 10
Delia, slave SUM 6
Delia, slave of David Maull EDG 3
Delila, slave MBO 4
Delila, slave of John Jenings EDG 10
Delk, Alpha BAR 11
Delorme, Anthony SUM 14
Delpha, slave MBO 3
Delphia, slave of J. J. Gilmer ABB 12
Delphy, slave of J. Watson ABB 10
Demaris, slave GRE 5
Dembeaux, slave ORA 8
Demby, Polly CFD 1
Dempsy, Elvi BAR 2
Denard, slave of Atticus Tucker EDG 4
Dendy, John EDG 14
Dendy, Marcus, slave of LAU 1
Dendy, William EDG 14
Dennis, slave UNI 3
Dennis, slave GRE 6
Dennis, slave SUM 13
Dennis, slave NEW 4
Dennis, Frances M. SUM 2
Dennis, Godsey E.WIL 2
Dennis, J. S. CHA 22
Dennis, Sarah S CHA 22
Derrick, Elisha NEW 4
Derrick, William NEW 4
Derry, slave SUM 6
Dennis, slave of John Tompkins EDG 17
Desassure, R. C. KER 2
DeSaussure, James, slave CHA 21
DeSaussure, John, slave CHA 21
Deveaux, J. P., slave of CHA 12
Deveaux, S., slaves of CHA 13
Devlin, J. J., slave of ABB 9
Devlin, James ABB 9
Devore, D. W., family of EDG 12
Devore, Elbert, slave of EDG 10
Devore, Luke EDG 9
Dewer, William S CHA 16
Dewes, Jonathan GRE 2
Dexter, Eliza C. CHA 15
Dial, Hastin, slave of LAU 1
Dial, Hastin, slaves of LAU 6-7
Diana, slave GRE 4
Diana, slave LAN 4
Diana, slave WIL 5
Diana, slave BAR 13
Diana, slave of F. A. Porcher CHA 2
Dianah, slave FAI 8
Dianna, slave COL 12
Dianna, slave COL 11
Dianna, slave GEO 2
Dianna, slave GEO 6
Diannah, slave ofBEA 1 Dr. William C. Daniels
Dice, slave UNI 5
Dicey, slave RIC 2
Dicey, slave NEW 8
Dick, slave DAR 2
Dick, slave DAR 2
Dick, slave DAR 3
Dick, slave UNI 4
Dick, slave UNI 5
Dick, slave LAN 1
Dick, slave COL 12
Dick, slave GEO 5
Dick, slave MRN 2
Dick, slave WIL 3
Dick, slave MBO 2
Dick, slave SUM 5

Dick, slave of Keating Ball CHA 2
Dick, slave of William Coleman EDG 19
Dick, slave of E. Dubose CHA 3
Dick, slave of Edmond Herndon PIC 6
Dick, slave of Robt Jennings EDG 13
Dick, slave of Robt Lamar EDG 14
Dick, slave of Dr. D. Legare CHA 6
Dick, slave of T. W. Porcher CHA 3
Dick, slave of EDG 19 Tilmon D. Purifoy
Dick, slave of John Thurman EDG 14
Dickerson, WilliamLEX 1
Dickert, Dolly NEW 5
Dickert, Dolly C NEW 7
Dickert, Lenora NEW 8
Dicks, Ann BAR 7
Dicks, Candless BAR 4
Dicks, Josias BAR 5
Dickson, David, slave of PIC 6
Dickson, ElizabethPIC 6
Dickson, John AND 7
Dickson, March, slave CHA 18
Dickson, Thomas C AND 4
Dido, slave BEA 12
Dido, slave COL 3
Die, slave BAR 14
Die, slave of Stephen Herren CHA 1
Dill, slave BAR 13
Dill, George F. GRE 8
Dillard, Alfred UNI 7
Dillard, Elvira LAU 5
Dillard, J. H., slaves of LAU 2
Dilsey, slave of Mat Morrus EDG 9
Dina, slave ORA 8
Dina, slave ORA 1
Dinah, slave DAR 1
Dinah, slave COL 8
Dinah, slave MBO 2
Dinah, slave ORA 1
Dinah, slave NEW 9
Dinah, slave ORA 2
Dinah, slave ORA 3
Dinah, slave SUM 7
Dinah, slave BAR 13
Dinah, slave of BEA 1 William D. Fitts
Dinah, slave of S. White CHA 1
Dinah, slave of L. C. Wilson ABB 7
Ditto, Saml, slave LAU 6
Dixon, Elizh., slave KER 1
Dobbins, James, child of AND 5
Dobbins, Nancy R AND 2
Dobbins, Polly SPA 4
Dobson, Francis CHA 17
Dobson, Oliver L CHA 17
Doby, J. S., family of EDG 11
Doby, John, slave EDG 16
Doby, Martha, slave of EDG 16
Dock, slave of T. B. Bird ABB 11
Doggarty, Persey CHA 16
Dogget, Mary CHA 20
Dohan, James CHA 23
Doll, slave of T. W. Porcher CHA 3
Dolly, slave GRE 1
Dolly, slave UNI 8
Dolly, slave BAR 2
Dolly, slave GEO 3
Donahoe, Michael CHA 18
Donald, Nancy J. ABB 14
Donaldson, James GRE 2
Donelson, Lydia ABB 15
Donn(?), William, slave of EDG 4
Donnalso, Isum (free black) ABB 8
Dora, slave SUM 14
Dorcas, slave WIL 2
Dorcas, slave MBO 4
Dorcas, slave UNI 6
Dorcas, slave of W. Barksdale ABB 13
Dorcas, slave of CHA 3 James Gaillard Sr.
Dorcas, slave of Susan Loveless EDG 3
Dorcas, slave of F. OConner EDG 6
Dorch, John BAR 9
Dormon, Benjamin HOR 2
Dorn, J., slaves of EDG 7
Dorn, Oliver, family of EDG 12
Dorn, William EDG 12
Dorroh, James LAU 8
Dorroh, Sarah, slave of LAU 8
Dorsey, slave GEO 6
Dorus, slave SUM 7
Douglas, Al., slaves of FAI 3
Douglas, Esther C CFD 1
Douglas, Isaac LAU 6
Douglas, Thos, slave KER 4
Douglas, William ORA 4
Douthit, Benjamin, slave of AND 3
Downing, Catherine M. WIL 2
Downing, Eliza BAR 12
Downing, Seth CHA 16
Dozier, Allen, slave of EDG 20
Dozier, Young EDG 18
Drafton, A. T. EDG 15
Drafton, A. T., slave of EDG 15
Drake, E. Sophia MBO 3
Draper, slave NEW 2
Drawdy, James W. COL 2
Drayton, Judy, CHA 16 slave
Drayton, Richard, slave CHA 16
Drayton, Rose, slave CHA 16
Dreher, Catherine LEX 2
Dreher, Rebeckah, slave LEX 2
Drennan, W. T., slaves of ABB 3
Drossey, slave of BEA 1 Major Henry Smart
Drucilla, slave NEW 2
Drucilla, slave UNI 8
Drury, slave COL 12
Dublin, slave of Thos Porcher Est.CHA 3
Dubose, C. C., slave of CHA 13
Dubose, E., slaves of CHA 3
DuBose, J. DAR 1
Dubose, S., slaves of FAI 1
Dubose, S., slave of CHA 2
Ducass, Wm., slaves of CHA 9
Duel, slave GEO 4
Duggins, Sarah FAI 2
Duke, slave WIL 5
Dukes, Mary A. WIL 4
Duncan, Allen PIC 4
Duncan, David GRE 4
Duncan, Elizabeth GRE 5
Dunkin, Mary HOR 1
Dunn, Emma J. HOR 3
Dunn, Lydia MBO 2
Dunn, Mary J. ABB 14
Dunn, Peter HOR 3
Dunn, Peter MBO 2
Dunn, W., slave of ABB 12
Duncan, William SPA 4
Dunmore, slave YRK 1
Dunnan, Hannah YRK 2
Dunning, Sanford CHA 25
Dunny, slave of Est. Thos PorcherCHA 3
Dunwoody, S., slave of ABB 16
Dupong, John BEA 10
Dupree, Revd D., slaves of CHA 11
Duquercrow, FrancesCHA 24
Durham, J., slave of FAI 8
Durham, Joel, slave of FAI 1
Duryea, J. S. CHA 21
Duvall, G. W., slave of CFD 2
Dye, Thos, slave KER 2
Dye, Mary A. KER 2

Eakins, B., slaves ABB 9
Eakins, William ABB 15
Eakins, William H ABB 9
Earle, E. J., slave of AND 5
Earle, Edward AND 8
Earle, Edward, slave of AND 8
Earle, Elias, slave of PIC 5
Earle, Harriet AND 9
Earle, J. B., slaves of AND 8
Earskin, Nancy AND 2
Easley, Adaline, slave PIC 1
Easley, Bob, slave PIC 1
Easley, George, slave PIC 1
East, William, slave of LAU 1

Easter, slave SPA 3
Easter, slave of John Simton FAI 3
Easter, slave of N. M. Strother ABB 5
Easther, slave SUM 2
Eaton, Joseph EDG 9
Eaves, Jackson BAR 12
Eban, slave of A. T. Miller ABB 15
Ebenezer, slave GRE 5
Ebin, slave UNI 8
Eddington, F. H., slave of FAI 3
Ede, slave of S. L. Marshall ABB 10
Edenfield, CharlesBAR 4
Ederington, J., slave of FAI 4
Edinfield, Wm. BAR 4
Edgar, slave SUM 8
Edgar, John T. PIC 5
Edge, James HOR 3
Edgeworth, RichardCFD 3 L., slave of
Edings, Sancho, slave BEA 8
Edings, Thos, slave BEA 8
Edmond, slave of EDG 4 J. M. C. Freeland
Edmond, slave EDG 2
Edmond, slave of J. W. Stokes EDG 2
Edmonds, S. E., slave of ABB 2
Edmund, slave LAN 2
Edmund, slave FAI 1
Edmund, slave NEW 9
Edmund, slave SUM 7
Edmund, slave of J. B. Richey ABB 15
Edmund, slave of J. Watson ABB 10
Edmunds, Jacob, slave RIC 1
Edmunds, Laura, slave RIC 1
Edmunds, Maria, slave RIC 1
Edmunds, Rozella, slave RIC 1
Edna, slave of J. Sall ABB 17
Edney, slave of O. Towles EDG 7
Edward, slave NEW 5
Edward, slave FAI 7
Edward, slave COL 2
Edward, slave COL 11
Edward, slave of M. Williamson FAI 8
Edward, Charles Thomas CFD 2
Edward, Wm. EDG 18
Edwards, A., slave of ABB 6
Edwards, John, slave of LAU 9
Edwards, Milley LAU 9
Edwin, slave WIL 5
Eigleburger, George A., slaves LEX 2
Eiza, slave ORA 9
Elay, slave WIL 1
Elbert, slave of Wiley Glover EDG 14
Elbert, slave of Mary Harrison EDG 16
Elbert, slave of Alex Sharpton EDG 15
Elbert, slave of H. C. Turner EDG 5
Elcy, slave SUM 2
Elcy, slave SUM 4
Elcy, slave SUM 8
Elder, James CHA 27
Eley, slave WIL 5
Elfa, slave ORA 1
Elgin, Hezekiah S AND 5
Eli, slave NEW 6
Eli, slave SUM 6
Elias, slave BAR 14
Elias, slave GEO 3
Elias, slave SPA 3
Elias, slave SPA 4
Elick, slave COL 10
Elijah, slave SUM 10
Elison, slave WIL 1
Elison, Matilda SUM 8
Eliza, slave BAR 4
Eliza, slave BAR 5
Eliza, slave BAR 5
Eliza, slave BAR 7
Eliza, slave GEO 4
Eliza, slave WIL 4
Eliza, slave SUM 1
Eliza, slave SUM 3
Eliza, slave SUM 11
Eliza, slave SUM 12
Eliza, slave UNI 5
Eliza, slave UNI 5
Eliza, slave GRE 1
Eliza, slave GRE 2
Eliza, slave of D. Harris EDG 5
Eliza, slave of J. S. Adams ABB 16
Eliza, slave of Joseph Adams EDG 17
Eliza, slave of J. Allston ABB 6
Eliza, slave of A. Edwards ABB 6
Eliza, slave of B. M. Cheatham ABB 12
Eliza, slave of S. Marshall ABB 10
Eliza, slave of WM. Mazyck CHA 11
Eliza, slave of Jonathan Mickle FAI 8
Eliza, slave of W. McCants CHA 6
Eliza, slave of B. McGee AND 1
Eliza, slave of H. M. Prince ABB 7
Eliza, slave of EDG 19 Joseph E. Rutherford
Eliza, slave of Jacob B. Smith EDG 18
Eliza, slave of A. Vance ABB 11
Elizabeth, slave NEW 7
Elizabeth, slave SUM 2
Elizabeth, slave of William T.GardnerEDG 14
Elizabeth, slave of Benja. Skren(?) EDG 9
Elizer, slave GEO 4
Elkins, infant slaves RIC 3
Elkins, Elliott, slaves of FAI 4
Elkins, Emily, slave FAI 4
Ella(?), slave GRE 7
Ella, slave of T. A. Conner ABB 16
Ella, slave of S. Dunwoody ABB 16
Ellen, slave BAR 11
Ellen, slave BAR 14
Ellen, slave FAI 2
Ellen, slave NEW 8
Ellen, slave ORA 8
Ellen, slave NEW 4
Ellen, slave COL 2
Ellen, slave YRK 2
Ellen, slave BEA 14
Ellen, slave GRE 3
Ellen, slave GRE 6
Ellen, slave GRE 7
Ellen, slave of Martha Doby EDG 16
Ellen, slave of J. S. Gibbs CHA 6
Ellen, slave of S. T. Gourdin CHA 13
Ellen, slave of William Mobley EDG 5
Ellenburg, John F.PIC 6
Ellerbe, Z., slave of CFD 2
Ellerson, C. E., slave of FAI 1
Ellick, slave CHA 12
Ellick, slave BAR 9
Ellick, slave of John Bausket EDG 5
Ellick, slave of J. Capeheart EDG 10
Ellick, slave of Elizabeth HibberEDG 10
Ellick, slave of William Holson EDG 6
Elliott, slave WIL 1
Elliott, Agnes, slave BEA 8
Elliott, Cyrus, slave BEA 8
Elliott, Harriet ORA 1
Elliott, Julia, slave BEA 8
Elliott, Juliet G CHA 19
Elliott, Mary B BEA 10
Elliott, Paddy, slave BEA 8
Elliott, Peggy, slave BEA 8
Elliott, Richey, slave of FAI 3
Elliott, T. R. S., slave BEA 14
Elliot, Wm. G. CHR 4
Ellis, slave SUM 10
Ellis, slave GEO 3
Ellis, Frank, slave CHA 19
Ellis, Franklin BEA 1
Ellis, Isaac, slave of BEA 14
Ellis, James, slave of UNI 1
Ellis, Joe, slave BEA 6
Ellis, Nathaniel B BEA 1
Ellis, Natt, slaves of BEA 2
Ellis, Rebecca BEA 1

Ellis, Rebecca BEA 1
Ellis, Roger, slave BEA 6
Ellis, Thomas, slave BEA 6
Ellison, slave SUM 1
Ellison, slave UNI 5
Ellison, Harriet M. SUM 8
Elmore, Stephen B ABB 10
Elp, Edward CHA 19
Elsa, slave of S. A. Tillman EDG 6
Elsey, slave COL 2
Elsey, slave GEO 8
Elsey, slave GEO 4
Elsey, slave COL 3
Elsey, slave GEO 8
Elsey, slave COL 2
Elsy, slave ORA 9
Elsy, slave BAR 9
Elvington, Gilas MRN 2
Elvira, slave ORA 3
Elvira, slave HOR 1
Elvy, slave of S. B. Brooks ABB 11
Elzy, slave BAR 11
Emaline, slave of J. Capeheart EDG 10
Emaline, slave of EDG 9
A. G. Hackett
Emamuel UNI 6
Emanuel, slave ORA 8
Emeline, slave FAI 8
Emeline, slave MBO 4
Emely, slave of L. Smith ABB 9
Emerie, slave COL 1
Emery, slave GRE 3
Emily, slave BAR 5
Emily, slave SUM 13
Emily, slave COL 11
Emily, slave of G. C. Mayson EDG 4
Emily, slave of H. C. Turner EDG 5
Emma, slave BAR 5
Emma, slave LAN 2
Emma, slave SUM 12
Emma, slave SUM 9
Emma, slave of H. Reece AND 1
Emma, slave of J. Vance ABB 17
Emmery(?), MildredORA 6
Emory, Edward, slave of PIC 6
England, AlexanderCHA 15
England, Henry, slave CHA 16
English, Rosanna, slave LEX 2
Enlson, slave BAR 11
Enoch, slave MBO 2
Enoch, slave of M. Ritchey ABB 12
Enslow, Catherine GRE 4
Enslow, Jacob GRE 4
Ephraim, slave UNI 4
Ephraim, slave of Mary Strains EDG 1
Epps, Jonas, slaves of LAU 7
Epsy, slave SUM 5
Epting, Eve NEW 8
Epting, David LEX 2
Epting, Ephrim LEX 2

Epting, Levi C. NEW 8
Era, slave BAR 1
Ergle, David EDG 10
Erwine, Ann B. YRK 3
Esau, slave of R. Robinson ABB 17
Ester, Susan, slave of FAI 3
Estes, George W. CHR 5
Estes, Wm. CHR 3
Esther, slave UNI 6
Esther, slave ORA 2
Esther, slave of D. Harris EDG 5
Esther, slave of E. Owen ABB 5
Esther, slave of Mewco Samuel EDG 16
Etherage, Noah EDG 19
Etheridge, Joel ABB 18
Eugenia, slave UNI 7
Eugenia, slave BAR 9
Eugenia, slave of M. Cannon ABB 2
Eustis, Ben, slave BEA 7
Eustis, Quash, slave BEA 7
Eustis, Saturday, slave BEA 7
Eustis, Tomas, slave BEA 7
Evaline, slave GRE 2
Evans, Ann E. SUM 11
Evans, Hannah KER 3
Evans, Harriet FAI 2
Evans, John FAI 2
Evans, Lear PIC 2
Evans, Robert CHA 20
Evans, Thomas GEO 9
Eve, slave NEW 8
Eve, slave NEW 5
Eve, slave of Dr. Palmer CHA 3
Eve, slave of CHA 1
Dr. T. G. Prioleau
Everett, John, slave of EDG 2

Fagan, Patrick CHA 17
Fagan, Sara MBO 2
Faine, slave FAI 7
Fair, slave COL 1
Fair, J., slaves of ABB 15
Fairis, Daniel ABB 5
Fairly, Sarah CFD 1
Fairy, John ORA 6
Falls, Malissa FAI 3
Fanney, slave of B. McGee AND 1
Fannie, slave of Samuel Sterling FAI 3
Fanny, slave GEO 8
Fanny, slave MBO 2
Fanny, slave NEW 3
Fanny, slave CHA 12
Fanny, slave BAR 8
Fanny, slave BAR 2
Fanny, slave BAR 10
Fanny, slave BAR 13
Fanny, slave SUM 11
Fanny, slave DAR 2
Fanny, slave YRK 1
Fanny, slave of D. Fant UNI 2

Fanny, slave of A. Giles ABB 8
Fanny, slave of Daniel Holland EDG 5
Fanny, slave of Matilda Jeter UNI 1
Fanny, slave of T. P. Lipscombe ABB 18
Fanny, slave of W. Means ABB 7
Fanny, slave of D. Morgan UNI 1
Fanny, slave of Joseph Shanklin PIC 5
Fanny, slave of R. Walker ABB 3
Fant, David, slave of UNI 2
Fant, Frances UNI 8
Fant, Julius F. AND 6
Fant, R. C. AND 6
Fany, slave SPA 4
Farley, W. B., slave of LAU 3
Farmer, Rupert SPA 3
Farr, Mrs. BEA 10
Farr, Mary P. BEA 11
Farr, R. H., slave ofUNI 1
Farris, Margaret YRK 1
Farris, Rachel C YRK 4
Farrow, Pattilo LAU 3
Fay, Jobn EDG 8
Fayssoux, Jane, slave CHA 26
Feagle, Laurens NEW 6
Feaster, J. C., slave of FAI 8
Feaster, J. F., slave of FAI 8
Featherston, John H FAI 2
Feb, slave BAR 10
Febby, slave BAR 13
Felix, slave BAR 13
Felix, slave of EDG 3
Douglas Robertson
Feller, Josiah E NEW 5
Fellows, John CHA 23
Felton, Martha AND 5
Fereby, slave of Benjn Coleman EDG 16
Fergason, Richard S., slave LAU 5
Fergoson, John (free black) LAU 7
Ferguson, Andrew, slave PIC 4
Ferguson, Mrs. Fanny COL 1
Ferguson, Jas. CHR 1
Ferguson, Jas., slave of CHA 1
Ferguson, John CHA 22
Ferguson, Nancy PIC 4
Ferguson, Robt GRE 4
Ferguson, S. CHR 1
Feriby, slave of M. H. Scurry EDG 10
Ferrill, Lesly MRN 1
Ferrill, Thomas F PIC 5
Ferry, slave GRE 8
Fertick, Mary LEX 3
Field, Henry CHA 17
Fielding, slave NEW 1
Fielding, slave of Jane E. Childs ABB 1

Fillpot, William C. ABB 18
Finley, Col., slave of FAI 4
Finley, Rebecca LAU 6
Finney, John, slave of LAU 1
Finse, James BAR 12
Fitspatrick, Edward CHA 25
Fitspatrick, John CHA 19
Fitts, Amelia EDG 2
Fitts, Eliza O. YRK 1
Fitts, William D., slave of BEA 1
Fitzgerrald, Eli PIC 2
Fitzjerald, Mary CHA 23
Flack, James E. GRE 5
Flander, slave SUM 12
Flander, slave SUM 1
Flann, W. A. LAN 3
Fleck, Jane NEW 2
Fleming, Dianah, slave CHA 24
Fleming, Margaret CHA 16
Fleming, William, slaves of LAU 5
Flora, slave COL 7
Flora, slave GEO 6
Flora, slave COL 8
Flora, slave BAR 3
Flora, slave BAR 3
Flowers, Ann E. SUM 14
Floyd, J., slaves of ABB 18
Floyd, Levi SUM 11
Floyd, Matilda NEW 3
Floyd, Sarah WIL 2
Floyd, Sarah YRK 5
Floyd, Wm. W. SUM 11
Floyed, Federick HOR 2
Floyed, Hugh J. HOR 2
Flogler, William G WIL 5
Fogartie, Isaac CHA 17
Fogle, Lewis ORA 2
Folk, C. M. E. NEW 8
Folk, Joanna NEW 8
Folley, William CHA 22
Fooshee, Charles ABB 18
Fooshee, William H. P. ABB 19
Force, L. M. CHA 22
Ford, Charlotte, slave KER 2
Ford, Barbary, slave CHA 15
Ford, Eliza BAR 10
Ford, John,slave KER 2
Ford, Richard D. CHA 17
Fore, Ann MRN 2
Foreman, Benj. BAR 7
Foreman, Mary BAR 7
Forgy, Asa, slaves ofLAU 6
Forrester, William, slave of BEA 1
Fortenberry, Thos KER 2
Fortesine, Cinthia A. ABB 4
Fortune, slave COL 11
Fortune, slave WIL 3
Fortune, slave COL 1
Fortune, slave WIL 1
Fortune, slave MRN 1
Fortune, Laodocia BAR 4
Fortune, Laura BAR 4
Foshee, Henry, slave of LAU 1
Foster, slave of D. Adkins ABB 9
Foster, Chas., slave of CHA 3
Foster, Edmund UNI 5
Foster, Edward UNI 3
Foster, Hetty N. LAU 8
Foster, Jemima UNI 7
Foster, M. A. SPA 3
Fowler, Frances UNI 3
Fowler, Francis HOR 2
Fowler, Franklin UNI 5
Fowler, Melinda UNI 3
Fowler, Melissa UNI 3
Fowler, Meredith LAU 5
Fowler, Meredith, slave of LAU 5
Fowler, Ramsay LAU 4
Fowler, Sarah LAU 1
Fowler, Tolopha UNI 4
Fox, Jesse LEX 3
Fox, John, slave LEX 1
Frace, slave of A. Huger CHA 7
France, slave GEO 1
Frances, slave SUM 3
Frances, slave of Joel Cose AND 1
Frances, slave of A. P. Couner ABB 5
Frances, slave of Wm. Culclazier EDG 3
Frances, slave of J. J. DevlinABB 9
Frances, slave of EDG 17 William J. Wightman
Francis, slave BEA 11
Francis, Sally KER 4
Frank, slave SPA 1
Frank, slave YRK 2
Frank, slave SUM 1
Frank, slave SUM 8
Frank, slave WIL 4
Frank, slave GEO 5
Frank, slave GEO 1
Frank, slave COL 2
Frank, slave ORA 3
Frank, slave UNI 7
Frank, slave of John Bauskett EDG 5
Frank, slave of J. P. Bodie EDG 18
Frank, slave of W. B. Brooks ABB 11
Frank, slave of BEA 2 Dr. William C. Daniels
Frank, slave of Elizabeth Hibber EDG 10
Frank, slave of Wyatt Holmes EDG 1
Frank, slave of Lucas Est. CHA 7
Frank, slave of Allen McFarland CFD 1
Frank, slave of Sallie Richardson EDG 10
Frankey, slave of N. Harris ABB 3
Franklin, infant NEW 1
Franklin, slave GEO 5
Franklin, D & L., slave of ABB 15
Franklin, Sarah ABB 15
Franklow, J. J. LEX 1
Franks, Allis LAU 6
Franks, Osker LAU 6
Fraser, Louisa BAR 4
Frasier, infant AND 3
Frasier, P. W. GEO 9
Frazer, S., slave of CHA 6
Fred, slave of Jane Kenneday FAI 8
Frederick, slave NEW 4
Fredrick, slave BAR 3
Frederick, slave of J. Allston ABB 6
Fredrick, Charles BAR 6
Freeland, J. M. C., slave of EDG 4
Freeman, H., slave of CHA 6
Freeman, Henry CHA 17
Freeman, Mary BEA 11
Freeman, Yancey, slave of EDG 13
Fretwell, J. Y., slave of AND 7
Fortune, Richard BAR 4
Friday, slave SUM 9
Friday, slave BEA 11
Friday, slave BAR 4
Friday, slave GEO 2
Friday, slave GEO 2
Friday, slave of Samuel Maxwell PIC 5
Fripp, Abner, slave BEA 9
Fripp, Amey, slave BEA 9
Fripp, Fatima, slave BEA 9
Fripp, Jackson, slave BEA 9
Fripp, Maria, slave BEA 9
Fripp, Michael, slave BEA 8
Fripp, Michael, slave BEA 7
Fripp, Oberon, slave BEA 7
Fripp, Quamina, slave BEA 6
Fripp, Richard, slave BEA 9
Fripp, Sarah, slave BEA 7
Fripp, Susey, slave BEA 9
Fripp, Thos, slaveBEA 9
Fripp, William, slave BEA 7
Fudge, Eliza J. CHR 3
Fudge, Minerva CHR 2
Fuller, Abel, slave BEA 9
Fuller, Agnes, slave BEA 9
Fuller, Agnes, slave BEA 9
Fuller, Alexr, slave BEA 9
Fuller, Barney, slave BEA 9
Fuller, Catharine CHA 15
Fuller, Catherine COL 11
Fuller, Charlotte, slave BEA 9
Fuller, James, slave BEA 9
Fuller, Jasper, slave BEA 9

Name	County	Page
Fuller, John R., infant of	LAU	3
Fuller, Mabel, slave	BEA	7
Fuller, Maria, slave	BEA	9
Fuller, Matinee J.	LAU	3
Fuller, Octavius, slave	BEA	9
Fuller, R. M., slave of	EDG	4
Fuller, Ransom, slaves of	LAU	3
Fuller, Sarah	COL	11
Fuller, Sunday, slave	BEA	9
Fuller, Toby, slave	BEA	9
Fuller, William, slaves of	BEA	14
Fuller, William	BEA	15
Fuller, William A., slave of	LAU	2
Funderburk, M. C.	LAN	3
Funderburk, N. A.	LAN	4
Furguson, Thos., slave of	EDG	13
Furman, slave	BAR	10
Furman, Harriet E	FAI	5
Furman, Thomas, slave of	FAI	4
Furse, James	BAR	4
Furtick, William	ORA	9
Gabriel, slave of H. Selana	CHA	6
Gadsden, slave	SUM	13
Gaillard, C. L., slaves of	AND	8
Gaillard, Dr., slave of	CHA	1
Gaillard, James Sr., slaves of	CHA	3
Gaillard, John K	AND	5
Gaines, E., slave of	ABB	11
Gains, W. H., slave	ABB	11
Galeway, William, slave	YRK	5
Gallishaw, Catharine	CHA	23
Galloway, Eliza	SUM	3
Gamant, John	YRK	1
Gambrell, Ira, slave of	AND	8
Gan(?), slave	GRE	8
Gantt, B.	ORA	5
Gantt, Hariet L.	ORA	2
Garantt, Josephus	NEW	2
Gardner, Eli R.	YRK	5
Gardener, Wm.	LAN	4
Gardner, William T., slaves of	EDG	14
Garet, slave	SUM	2
Garey, T. R., slave of	ABB	16
Garmany, William	NEW	4
Garner, infant	UNI	4
Garner, infant slaves	RIC	2
Garner, infant slaves	RIC	3
Garner, Sydney	EDG	10
Garret, slave of P. N. Acker	AND	4
Garret, Elizabeth, slave of	EDG	1
Garrett, slave of	EDG	16
Garrett, Harriet	GRE	2
Garrett, John	GRE	2
Garrett, John	PIC	6
Garrett, Thomas	UNI	7
Garrett, Thomas, slave of	EDG	1
Garrett, Tillman	AND	7
Garrett, Wm., slave of	EDG	15
Garrity, Margaret	CHA	22
Garvin, Melinda	PIC	4
Gary, Charles, slave of	LAU	2
Gaskins, Margaret	EWIL	2
Gaston, Wm	CHR	5
Gates, Margret	LEX	4
Gauntt, James	ORA	2
Gay, Henry	MBO	3
Gay, William	EDG	11
Gayden, Elijah, slaves of	FAI	8
Gayle, C. N.	SUM	14
Gaylord, Wm. A.	SUM	13
Geam, M. E.	KER	1
Gearin, Bill, slave	PIC	4
Gearin, Condes, slave	PIC	4
Gearin, Westly, slave	PIC	4
Geiger, John C., slaves	LEX	4
Geiger, Nancy, slaves	LEX	4
Geiger, Philip	LEX	2
Geiger, W. W., slaves of	EDG	16
Geiger, William, slaves	LEX	3
General, slave	NEW	4
General, slave of John T. Mitchell	EDG	19
Gennings, William	SPA	4
Gent, D., slave of	ABB	14
Gent, Jesse	ABB	14
Gentry, Elizabeth	AND	7
Gentry, William, child of	AND	9
George, slave	BAR	2
George, slave	BAR	2
George, slave	BAR	5
George, slave	BAR	11
George, slave	WIL	4
George, slave	COL	12
George, slave	COL	3
George, slave	GEO	3
George, slave	HOR	3
George, slave	HOR	3
George, slave	SUM	1
George, slave	SPA	1
George, slave	SPA	4
George, slave	YRK	3
George, slave	BEA	13
George, slave	GRE	4
George, slave	GRE	2
George, slave	GRE	1
George, slave(?)	LAN	3
George, slave	UNI	3
George, slave	UNI	6
George, slave	ORA	4
George, slave	ORA	1
George, slave	FAI	6
George, slave	NEW	9
George, slave of B. Blackaby	ABB	19
George, slave of Wosela Blalock	EDG	9
George, slave of Mary Birtt	ABB	1
George, slave of H. Clark	ABB	18
George, slave of M. W. Clary	EDG	4
George, slave of J. Cockrel	FAI	3
George, slave of Elbert Devore	EDG	10
George, slave of B. Eakins	ABB	9
George, slave of Richey Elliott	FAI	3
George, slave of R. H. Farr	UNI	1
George, slave of Caleb Holley	EDG	11
George, slave of Mary Holliway	EDG	4
George, slave of Edwd D. Jerman	CHA	9
George, slave of Jesse Jeter	UNI	2
George, slave of S. W. Jones	ABB	12
George, slave of Felix Lake	EDG	6
George, slave of W. Morrison	ABB	9
George, slave of Newman Mosly(?)	EDG	13
George, slave of S. W. Nicholson	EDG	6
George, slave of Sarah Pace	ABB	12
George, slave of T. W. Peyre	CHA	4
George, slave of Saml Porcher	CHA	13
George, slave of M. Roberts	AND	2
George, slave of J. Speer	ABB	13
George, John (mulatto)	COL	2
George, M. L. (free mulatto)	KER	4
George, Nelson	BAR	10
Georgiana, slave	BAR	3
Gerald, Jack, slave	KER	4
Gerald, Richd S	SUM	3
Gerry, slave	LAN	2
Gettys, M. L.	LAN	2
Getzer, George, slave of	EDG	15
Gevin, slave	BAR	12
Ghristee, Sophia Ann	GEO	5
Gibbert, Jeremiah	ABB	3
Gibbes, Cupid, slave	BEA	6
Gibbes, Shafto, slave	BEA	6
Gibbs, Fanny, slave	CHA	17
Gibbs, George, slave	CHA	17
Gibbs, J. S., slaves of	CHA	6
Gibbs, Joseph	CHA	17

Gibert, P., slave of ABB 12
Gibson, Amanda NEW 3
Gibson, Denis LEX 1
Gibson, Elizabeth, slave of EDG 19
Gibson, Louisa GRE 4
Gibson, Mary NEW 3
Gibson, Polodore, slave CHA 19
Gibson, R. CHR 1
Gibson, Sam, slave CHA 19
Gicey, slave NEW 1
Gilbert, slave HOR 2
Gilbert, slave GEO 6
Gilbert,slave GEO 1
Gilbert, slave of A. J. Logan ABB 9
Gilbert, slave of G. McDuffie ABB 13
Gilbert, Francis CHA 19
Gilchrist, Dempsey EDG 13
Gilchrist, Frank, slave CHA 19
Giles, slave of M. Buckhalter EDG 8
Giles, A., slaves of ABB 8
Giles, Chase, slave CHA 16
Giles, Francis, slave CHA 16
Gill, slave of Jas Blackwell EDG 11
Gillam, Cherry BAR 11
Gillam, George G. ABB 19
Gillam, Thos BAR 11
Gillard, Miss H., slaves of CHA 3
Gilles, slave WIL 1
Gillespie, Jane C ABB 7
Gillmore, S(?). D., slave LEX 1
Gilmer, J. J., slave of ABB 12
Gilmer, Nancy ABB 12
Gilmer, Susanna N. E. AND 9
Ginney, slave DAR 1
Ginney, slave DAR 4
Ginny, slave BAR 13
Ginny, slave of J. Pringle Smith BEA 5
Gipson, Emery GRE 6
Gist, John UNI 1
Gist, Sarah, slave of UNI 2
Givins, infant AND 3
Gladden, Minor, slave of FAI 1
Glascow, slave GEO 5
Glauger, N., family of EDG 5
Glaugier, Emma EDG 5
Glenn, slave ORA 9
Glenn, H. A., slave of FAI 4
Glenn, J. M. FAI 4
Glenn, Martha LAU 2
Glenn, Rachel GRE 3
Glover, Betsy, slave CHA 22
Glover, C. G., family of EDG 11
Glover, Henrietta ORA 2
Glover, John slave of FAI 3
Glover, John J. YRK 3
Glover, Martha J. YRK 3
Glover, Wiley, EDG 14
Glover, William YRK 3
Godber, Wm. G. CHA 5
Godman, Stillee LAU 3
Goettee, Washington, slave of BEA 1
Goff, slave BAR 9
Gohens, Roselina CHA 20
Gohens, Theodore CHA 20
Golding, Elisha NEW 3
Golding, Henry L. LAU 8
Goldings, Richard, slave of LAU 1
Goldtrap, Eliza CHA 23
Goodman, Hannah EDG 1
Goodwyn, Lucy, slave of FAI 5
Goodwyn, Tenah, slave RIC 1
Googler, Sally LEX 1
Gorden, Margaret J. ABB 15
Gordon, Harriet (free mulatto) CHA 25
Gordon, William (free mulatto) CHA 25
Gosten, Henry W., slave of LAU 3
Gore, Francis C. HOR 2
Goswick, Joseph UNI 7
Gourdin, S. T., slaves of CHA 13
Goven, F. G. EDG 11
Gower, William H. GRE 8
Grace, slave CHA 5
Grace, slave SUM 5
Grace, slave FAI 7
Grace, slave SUM 8
Grace, slave MBO 3
Grace, slave MBO 1
Grace, slave of H. W. Ledbetter ABB 16
Grace, slave of John Maxwell PIC 5
Grace, slave of T. W. Porcher CHA 3
Grace, slave of R. W. Watson FAI 3
Gracey, slave GRE 3
Gracey, slave of J. Holland ABB 19
Graham, Elizabeth HOR 3
Graham, Martha UNI 5
Grandeson, slave YRK 1
Grangar(?), Mary HOR 2
Granger, Samuel HOR 3
Granger, Riney HOR 3
Grant, Isaac E. LAU 6
Grasty, M. L., slave of EDG 2
Graves, Dr., slave of CHA 12
Graves, Eleanor COL 2
Graves, Emily CHA 20
Graves, G., slaves of ABB 13
Graves, Martha CHA 20
Graves, J. P., slave of ABB 3
Graves, Nat CHA 20
Graves, R. N., slave of ABB 13
Gray, Charles (free mulatto) CHA 26
Gray, Ezekiah,slaveLAU 5
Gray, Matilda MBO 3
Gray, Nat, slave CHA 19
Gray, Phillis, slave CHA 21
Gray, William (free mulatto) CHA 26
Grayham, Francis CABB 17
Grayham, Thomas A ABB 16
Grayham, James J. ABB 17
Grayson, ElizabethLAU 8
Grayson, Mathew LAU 8
Grayson, Milley, slave BEA 6
Grayson, Roger, slave BEA 6
Grayson, Toney, slave BEA 6
Gregg, H., slave of AND 5
Green, slave LAN 2
Green, slave of William Webb AND 4
Green, George BAR 5
Green, John CHA 22
Green, Pinckney GRE 4
Green, Polly SPA 1
Green, Sarah SUM 12
Green, Weathers FAI 6
Green, Wm. W. SUM 6
Greenoch, slave of Willis AlsobrookCFD 3
Greenwood, Eliza-beth PIC 5
Greer, Lettis AND 1
Gregg, David, slave of CFD 2
Gregg, Matilda AND 9
Gergorie, A. F., slaves BEA 15
Gregorie, James, slave of CHA 6
Gregory, J., slaves of UNI 1
Gregory, Thomas, slave of UNI 1
Gregory, William UNI 6
Gressett, Samuel R ORA 6
Grice, Thos EDG 18
Griffen, Jane MRN 3
Griffin, slave NEW 9
Griffin, A., slave of ABB 17
Griffin, Frances LAU 7
Griffin, Frances S. NEW 3
Griffin, J. C., slave of AND 6
Griffin, Jackson, slave of LAU 3
Griffin, Joseph LAU 3
Griffin, L., slave of ABB 16
Griffin, Margaret, slave of LAU 1
Griffin, N. L., family of EDG 11
Griffin, Nancy AND 2
Griffin, Richard, slave of EDG 7
Griffin, T. C., slave of ABB 16
Griffin, V. Est., slaves of ABB 10
Griffis, David LEX 1
Griffith, Jeffer-son NEW 1

Griggs, Margaret CFD 1
Growes, Caroline COL 5
Grubbs, Margaret FAI 5
Grubbs, Wood FAI 5
Guerrard, J. H., slaves of BEA 2
Guignard--see Guingyard LEX 4
Guignard, Jas S., slave of EDG 4
Guingyard, James S., slave LEX 4
Guingyard, James S. Jr., slaves LEX 4
Guiton, Elizabeth HOR 2
Gunter, A. ORA 4
Gunter, D. ORA 5
Gus, slave of T. P. Lipscombe ABB 18

Habernich, Arlet Crom CHA 15
Hacket, Lydia CHA 22
Hackett, A. G., slave of EDG 9
Hackett, M., slaves of ABB 11
Hackit, Isabella ABB 16
Hadly, William EDG 2
Hagah, slave GEO 2
Hagar, slave GEO 4
Hagar, slave COL 12
Hagar, slave GEO 5
Hagar, slave GEO 6
Hagar, slave COL 4
Hager, slave SUM 2
Hager, slave SUM 5
Hagar, slave of R. Laurens CHA 7
Hagood, Rachel BAR 2
Haines, James, slave CHA 25
Hair, child BAR 5
Hal, slave of H. Bolware EDG 5
Haley, Mary SUM 2
Hall, slave of John Coleman EDG 19
Hall, George T. ABB 8
Hall, H. SPA 4
Hall, James SPA 4
Hall, Jos. E., slaves of FAI 2
Hall, Lemuel, slave of AND 6
Hall, Mary F. ABB 8
Hall, Moultrie (free mulatto) CHA 26
Hall, Susannah SUM 2
Hallonquist, Mary BAR 8
Ham, slave COL 6
Hamby, Sarah GRE 1
Hamby, Sarah A. J. AND 2
Hamer, Edgar MRN 2
Hamer, Tristram MRN 3
Hamilton, slave SUM 4
Hamilton, D. Clinch, slaves ofBEA 2
Hamilton, Daniel CHA 22
Hamilton, ElisabethEDG 9
Hamilton, ElisabethEDG 12
Hamilton, Hannah, slave PIC 4
Hamilton, Hannah EDG 6
Hamilton, Thomas W AND 3
Hamlet, slave SUM 1
Hamlin, Miss, slave of CHA 6
Hammond, J. G., slave of EDG 15
Hammond, Sarah, slave of EDG 15
Hampton, slave BAR 6
Hampton, slave BAR 7
Hampton, Elizabeth MRN 3
Hanahan, John M. COL 11
Handy, slave BAR 8
Hane, Raichel, slave LEX 4
Haney, slave NEW 6
Haney, Oratio EDG 3
Haney, Stephen, child of AND 6
Hanks, George R. AND 1
Hanna, slave SUM 11
Hannah, slave BAR 10
Hannah, slave BAR 2
Hannah, slave NEW 6
Hannah, slave NEW 10
Hannah, slave NEW 2
Hannah, slave FAI 2
Hannah, slave ORA 5
Hannah, slave ORA 9
Hannah, slave BEA 11
Hannah, slave BEA 12
Hannah, slave DAR 1
Hannah, slave GRE 2
Hannah, slave GRE 1
Hannah, slave UNI 4
Hannah, slave SUM 12
Hannah, slave SUM 14
Hannah, slave COL 8
Hannah, slave COL 12
Hannah, slave WIL 4
Hannah, slave COL 8
Hannah, slave GEO 5
Hannah, slave HOR 2
Hannah, slave GEO 3
Hannah, slave RIC 2
Hannah, slave MRN 3
Hannah, slave MBO 1
Hannah, slave WIL 3
Hannah, slave of Z. V. Barnes ABB 5
Hannah, slave of J. Brownlee ABB 8
Hannah, slave of E. Covin ABB 3
Hannah, slave of S. Frazer CHA 6
Hannah, slave of H. Freeman CHA 6
Hannah, slave of J. Gregory UNI 1
Hannah, slave of Allen McFarland CFD 1
Hannah, W. J., slave of CFD 1
Hannahan, H. V. CHA 21
Hannibald, slave SUM 1
Hanschild, Jane CHA 22
Harvin, Thomas W., slave of PIC 5
Hardee, Sarah HOR 2
Harden, Jasper EDG 14
Hardenia, slave BAR 14
Hardenia, slave BAR 11
Hardtimes, slave GEO 6
Hardy, slave BAR 14
Hardy, slave UNI 6
Hardy, slave GEO 2
Hardy, slave COL 5
Hardy, Mary AND 9
Hardy, Sarah UNI 4
Hardy, William J. EDG 12
Hardy, R., family of EDG 12
Hariet, slave NEW 1
Hariet, slave of M. E. Hollingsworth EDG 12
Harkins, Jno GRE 5
Harkins, Rachel GRE 5
Harkins, Wm GRE 5
Harkless, slave BAR 3
Harkless, slave GRE 3
Harkness, John J. ABB 8
Harkness, Martha J. ABB 8
Harkness, Mary ABB 8
Harleston, J., slaves of CHA 7
Harley, slave BAR 5
Harling, James J ABB 1
Harlow, slave COL 4
Harlow, slave of S. S. Palmer CHA 9
Harmon, Nathinal LEX 2
Harper, slave EDG 16
Harper, J., slave of ABB 13
Harper, James, slaves of FAI 8
Harper, Lindsay ABB 13
Harper, Martha AND 3
Harrelson, M. E. GEO 5
Harriet, slave BAR 13
Harriet, slave BAR 11
Harriet, slave COL 8
Harriet, slave COL 6
Harriet, slave NEW 7
Harriet, slave NEW 9
Harriet, slave NEW 3
Harriet, slave NEW 10
Harriet, slave LAN 2
Harriet, slave GRE 2
Harriet, slave GRE 6
Harriet, slave YRK 1
Harriet, slave MBO 4
Harriet, slave MBO 2
Harriet, slave SUM 7
Harriet, slave of John Adams EDG 1
Harriet, slave of E. Calhoun ABB 3
Harriet, slave of N. J. Davis ABB 5
Harriet, slave of WM. Garrett EDG 15
Harriet, slave of W. W. Geiger EDG 16
Harriet, slave of E. Noble ABB 6
Harriet, slave of William PrescottEDG 16
Harriet, slave of W. C. Robertson EDG 4
Harriet, slave of Susan A. Roper EDG 16
Harriet, slave of E. Sproul ABB 9
Harriet, slave of H. C. Turner EDG 5
Harriet, slave of A. Vance ABB 11
Harriett, slave WIL 5
Harris, A., slaves of ABB 18
Harris, A., slave of ABB 4

Harris, C. LAN 1
Harris, D., family of EDG 5
Harris, David, family of EDG 5
Harris, Elizabeth EDG 9
Harris, Josephine NEW 2
Harris, Joshua AND 9
Harris, Milly, slave of ABB 4
Harris, N., slave of ABB 3
Harris, Nancy SPA 4
Harris(?), Pickens EDG 4
Harris, Pleasant UNI 1
Harris, Tom, slave CHA 21
Harris, William UNI 1
Harris, Z., slaves of EDG 4
Harris, Z., slaves of EDG 13
Harrison, slave SUM 7
Harrison, slave UNI 5
Harrison, slave NEW 4
Harrison, slave NEW 10
Harrison, slave of F. Scaife UNI 1
Harrison, John EDG 16
Harrison, John, slave of FAI 2
Harrison, John, slave of FAI 5
Harrison, Mary, slaves of EDG 16
Harrison, Wiley, slaves of EDG 16
Harrod, Jacintha BAR 3
Harrod(?), Susan BAR 3
Harry, slave BAR 11
Harry, slave CHA 12
Harry, slave ORA 3
Harry, slave ORA 4
Harry, slave ORA 3
Harry, slave BEA 12
Harry, slave COL 3
Harry, slave WIL 4
Harry, slave COL 5
Harry, slave COL 6
Harry, slave COL 6
Harry, slave SUM 3
Harry, slave SUM 5
Harry, slave of Keating Ball CHA 2
Harry, slave of S. C. Feaster FAI 8
Harry, slave of Dr. Gaillard CHA 1
Harry, slave of Martha Hobbs EDG 4
Harry, slave of Matilda Jeter UNI 1
Harry, slave of D. Mobley FAI 8
Harry, slave of Hugh Mosley EDG 10
Harry, slave of James McCrorey FAI 8
Harry, slave of S. S. Palmer CHA 9
Harry, slave of William J. Rountree EDG 14
Harry, slave of R. C. Sharp ABB 12
Harry, slave of K. Simmes Sr. CHA 1
Hart, Franklin EDG 5
Hart, Levina ORA 4
Hartpens, Mary CHA 18
Hartzog, Susan BAR 6
Harverson, Robt CHA 12
Harvey, slave AND 3
Harvey, slave MRN 3
Harvin, Neoma SUM 4
Harvy, slave BEA 12
Haselden, L., slave of CHA 6
Haseltine, slave NEW 4
Haskell, W. C., slave of ABB 7
Haskill, T. C., slaves of ABB 17
Hatcher, Benjn, slave of EDG 16
Hatcher, John FAI 3
Hauck, John H. CHA 19
Haw, slave COL 10
Hawkins, AND 1
Hawkins, Catherine GRE 5
Hawkins, Marshal GRE 1
Hawkins, Nathan UNI 1
Hawthorn, Robert, slave of FAI 5
Hawthorne, P. O., slave of ABB 12
Hawthorne, Sany ABB 12
Hay, Fredrick BAR 2
Hay, John UNI 7
Hay, R. W., slave of ABB 7
Haygood, B., slave of FAI 8
Haynes, Benj. BAR 7
Hays, J. C., slave of ABB 4
Hays, Joseph MRN 3
Hazard, slave of A. A. Houston ABB 4
Hazard, slave of A. Houston ABB 3
Hazel, Richard LAU 1
Hazel, Sam, slave BEA 6
Head, Saml EDG 6
Hearn, Keran, slave of EDG 17
Heath, Laura A. FAI 6
Hector, slave BAR 11
Hector, slave SUM 8
Hector, slave ORA 8
Hector, slave BEA 11
Hector, slave of Mary Butler EDG 2
Hector, slave of T. W. Porcher CHA 3
Hefferman, Francis ABB 17
Hefferman, Sarah M. ABB 17
Hefron, Henry P. CHA 20
Hefron, Margaret CHA 20
Hellams, George LAU 8
Hembree, James AND 7
Hemminger, Jeannette ABB 3
Hemphill, William M. ABB 14
Henderson, slave YRK 2
Henderson, Barbra LAU 8
Henderson, George R. CHA 19
Henderson, Henry LAU 8
Henderson, James C., slave LAU 6
Henderson, James L ABB 7
Henderson, Jane LAU 8
Henderson, John LAU 8
Henderson, John S. LAU 2
Henderson, Sarah PIC 2
Henderson, Thomas P. CFD 1
Hendrex, Leroy, slave LEX 1
Hendrick, William, slave of CFD 3
Hendricks, E. DAR 3
Hendricks, J. DAR 1
Hendricks, Thos, slaves of LAU 6
Hendrix, Henry, slave LEX 1
Hendrix, Jacob LEX 1
Hendrix, James H. PIC 4
Hendrix, Perry SPA 1
Hendrix, Toney, slave PIC 4
Henning, J. G. GEO 9
Hennings, N. B., slave of CHA 6
Henrietta, slave SUM 9
Henrietta, slave of Wm. Nevil AND 1
Henry, slave SUM 3
Henry, slave SUM 14
Henry, slave SUM 8
Henry, slave SUM 10
Henry, slave GEO 5
Henry, slave WIL 2
Henry, slave GEO 5
Henry, slave NEW 2
Henry, slave NEW 4
Henry, slave NEW 5
Henry, slave NEW 9
Henry, slave NEW 6
Henry, slave NEW 8
Henry, slave FAI 8
Henry, slave ORA 9
Henry, slave SUM 13
Henry, slave UNI 8
Henry, slave UNI 6
Henry, slave GRE 2
Henry, slave GRE 1
Henry, slave GRE 7
Henry, slave GRE 8
Henry, slave BAR 8
Henry, slave BAR 2
Henry, slave CHA 14
Henry, slave of S. Banks FAI 3
Henry, slave of J.P. Barrot ABB 10
Henry, slave of A. P. Couner ABB 5
Henry, slave of Richard L. Edgeworth CFD 3
Henry, slave of A. Hill FAI 6
Henry, slave of A. Houston ABB 3
Henry, slave of Robt Jennings EDG 13
Henry, slave of Robt D. Killin CFD 1
Henry, slave of D. R. Sartor UNI 1
Henry, slave of W. Templeton ABB 17
Henry, slave of John Thurman EDG 14

Henry, slave of B. H. Watson ABB 17
Henry, slave of J. Watson ABB 10
Henry, slave of W. Wilson ABB 12
Henry, C. H. CHR 2
Henry, Frances(?), free black YRK 5
Henry, James E. SPA 3
Henry, James T. ABB 15
Henson, slave NEW 8
Henson, slve of John Lyons EDG 11
Henson, J. R. NEW 3
Henson, S. A. KER 4
Hepney, slave SUM 3
Hercules COL 6
Hercules, slave COL 1
Herdon, Sarah CHA 27
Heriet, slave GEO 2
Heriet, slave GEO 5
Herman, Andrew CHA 18
Hemrby, Joseph PIC 5
Herndon,Edmond, slave of PIC 6
Herndon,Mary NEW 9
Herren, Stephen, slave of CHA 1
Herrin, J., slave of EDG 18
Hester, slave BAR 12
Hester, slave SUM 7
Hester, slave SUM 10
Hester, slave MRN 3
Hester, slave GEO 3
Hester, slave WIL 3
Hester, slave BEA 12
Hester, slave of Charles Packman EDG 1
Hester, James PIC 6
Hester, Luvina PIC 2
Hesther, slave ORA 9
Hetty, slave COL 10
Heuff, Jos. W. CHA 12
Hewit, Maria CHA 6
Heyward, Nathaniel, slaves ofBEA 14
Hibber, Elizabeth, slaves of EDG 10
Hibler, Charles J.EDG 10
Hibler, Isaac A., slave of EDG 2
Hicklin, ZachariahCHR 2
Hickman, Pinckney SUM 12
Hicks, Danl SUM 11
Hicks, Jesse WIL 2
Hicks, Lusinder C.LEX 1
Hicks, Osborn COL 6
Hicks, Robert N., slave of CFD 2
Hide, Jeremiah GRE 6
Hightower, J., slave of EDG 14
Hiliard, slave of S. B. Brooks ABB 11
Hill, A., slave of FAI 6
Hill, Anna, CHA 12
Hill, E., slave of FAI 6
Hill, Elizabeth LAU 1
Hill, Frances ABB 8
Hill, J. P., slaves of UNI 1
Hill, Jas. W. SUM 4
Hill, John F. LAU 5
Hill, John J., infant of LAU 2
Hill, John J., infant of LAU 2
Hill, John J., slave of LAU 2
Hill, Josephine ORA 6
Hill, Julian EDG 12
Hill, Margaret E. LAU 1
Hill, Mary R. UNI 1
Hill, T. C., slave of AND 5
Hill, Thos, family of EDG 12
Hill, Thos, slaves of EDG 18
Hill, Wiley, slaves of LAU 5
Hill, William EDG 2
Hillard, A. G. KER 2
Hiller, George C. NEW 4
Hillery, slave NEW 5
Hillery, slave of J. H. Wideman ABB 1
Hilliard, slave ORA 2
Hilliard, slave YRK 3
Hillin, slave of M. Roberts AND 2
Hilton, Emeline COL 5
Hilton, John J. SUM 2
Hind, Rester MRN 1
Hindman, A. N., slaves of FAI 8
Hindman, John CHR 1
Hindman, Mary A. FAI 6
Hindman, Sarah FAI 8
Hinds, Enealy MRN 3
Hines, Littlebury SPA 4
Hinnant, Josiah, slaves of FAI 3
Hinnant, Mary FAI 4
Hipp, Margaret NEW 9
Hitch, John LAU 2
Hitchfield, Wilm. CHA 21
Hitt, Giney LAU 2
Hitton, William LAN 3
Hobbs, Martha, slave of EDG 4
Hobson, Sicily, slave of UNI 1
Hodges, John GRE 5
Hoff,Daniel CHA 12
Hogarth, Thomas BEA 14
Hogg AND 1
Hogg, James W. NEW 5
Holaway, Sarah GRE 1
Holcombe, Minor PIC 4
Holder, Elizabeth GRE 5
Holeman, Isabel R LEX 1
Holland, Daniel EDG 5
Holland, J, slaves of ABB 19
Holland, Joseph, slave CHA 24
Holland, Mary AND 8
Holland, Thomas LAU 2
Holleman, R. S., slave of ABB 8
Holley, Caleb, family of EDG 11
Holleyman, John, slave KER 4
Holleyman, W., slave KER 4
Holliday, Martha A. SUM 2
Holliday, Temperance SUM 4
Hollingsworth, B., slave of EDG 11
Hollingsworth, M. E., family of EDG 12
Hollingsworth, slave of EDG 16
Holliway, Jordan, slaves of EDG 12
Holliway, Levi G., slave of EDG 4
Holliway, Mary EDG 3
Holliway, Mary, slave of EDG 4
Holliway, Perry EDG 4
Holliway, Perry, slave of EDG 4
Holmes, Amos, slave of EDG 3
Holmes, Emily EDG 11
Holmes, G. P., slave of LAU 7
Holmes, John B. EDG 11
Holmes, John G., family of EDG 6
Holmes, Lavina (free mulatto) CHA 26
Holmes, Margaret A.FAI 7
Holmes, Peter, slave CHA 25
Holmes, Shade, slave of EDG 1
Holmes, Wm. EDG 11
Holmes, Wm., slave of EDG 11
Holmes, William EDG 1
Holmes, Wyatt EDG 1
Holmes, Wyatt, slave of EDG 1
Holson, Elizabeth EDG 1
Holson, Martha EDG 1
Holson, William, slave of EDG 6
Holsonback, Eliza EDG 3
Holsten, Wade, slave of EDG 18
Holstun, Mary EDG 18
Holstun, Moses, slave of EDG 19
Holt, Isabell ABB 18
Holtano, Bennett, slave of EDG 20
Homes, Wm., slave of AND 2
Hood, A. LAN 2
Hood, J. LAN 2
Hood, Jesse YRK 4
Hood, Jordan AND 2
Hood, M. LAN 2
Hooker, Mary GRE 4
Hope, John C., slave LEX 2
Hope, Mary YRK 2
Hopkins, James S. PIC 1
Horger, Elizabeth ORA 8
Horlbeck, Bob, slave CHA 20
Horn, slave SPA 1
Horne, Rob. C. SUM 11
Hornet, slave NEW 3
Horris, slave HOR 1
Horry, Charles, slave CHA 21
Horry, Luke, slave CHA 21
Horst, J. W., slave of ABB 1
Horton, H. LAN 4
Houck, E. ORA 8

Hough, Mary CFD 1
House, K. KER 4
Houston, A., slaves of ABB 3
Houston, A. A., slave of ABB 4
Houze, J. LAN 3
Howard, slave SPA 3
Howard, Elbert P EDG 3
Howard, Green EDG 3
Howard, Robert CHA 18
Howel, Sarah GEO 6
Howel, slave BAR 14
Howel, John J., slave LEX 3
Howell, Sarah CHR 3
Howell, Solomon GRE 4
Howen, Eliz. J. SUM 1
Hubert, Catharine CHA 16
Huckale, G. W., slave of ABB 8
Huff, James D., slave LEX 3
Huff, Mary GRE 6
Huffman, Lucretia EDG 1
Huger, A., slaves of CHA 7
Huger, Ann, slave CHA 21
Huger, B., slaves of ABB 8
Huger, Harriet CHA 15
Huger, Pompey, slave CHA 15
Huggins, Seneth MRN 2
Huggins, Charles GEO 9
Hughes, A. E. PIC 2
Hughes, Harriet LAU 9
Hughes, J. H., family of EDG 6
Hughes, John ABB 6
Hughes, M. DAR 4
Hughes, Martha, slave of ABB 6
Hughes, William D PIC 6
Hughey, J., slave of ABB 9
Hughey, V., slave of ABB 9
Hughs, E. ORA 3
Hugins, J. DAR 3
Huguenin, C. J., slaves of BEA 14
Hulda, slave of S. Marshall ABB 10
Hull, Mrs. L. CHA 9
Hume, Gadsden CHA 24
Hume, Mariah CHA 24
Hume, Mary AND 7
Humphrey, slave NEW 6
Humphrey, William GRE 2
Humphreys, Wm. M. AND 5
Humphries, Jas C BAR 3
Humphries, Thomas B. ABB 4
Hunt, Ann PIC 2
Hunt, Ben, slave PIC 1
Hunt, Fanning PIC 1
Hunt, Henson PIC 1
Hunt, Jane, slave PIC 1
Hunt, Jane PIC 1
Hunt, Mary PIC 1
Hunt, Mason PIC 1
Hunt, Rachael, slave PIC 1
Hunter, A., slaves of ABB 8
Hunter, A. A., slave of ABB 12
Hunter, Elizabeth NEW 4
Hunter, Mary, slaves of LAU 5
Hunter, Wm., slave of LAU 5
Hurlong, H. C., slaves of EDG 2
Hustess, Mary CFD 2
Hutchet, John CHA 20
Hutchet, Phebe CHA 20
Hutchinson, M., slaves of ABB 18
Hutson, Danl COL 8
Hutson, Dr. Hu W., slaves BEA 15
Hutson, Mrs. Martha, slave BEA 15
Hutto, Amy ORA 4
Hutto, Careline LEX 3
Hutto, Eliza ORA 4
Hutto, James M. BAR 13
Hutto, Wm. BAR 4
Hutto, William ORA 2
Hyer, Henry CHA 18

Icas, slave LAN 3
Ide, Joseph J. YRK 1
Inabnit, Uriah, slaves of EDG 18
Indy, slave ORA 8
Infinger, Harriet COL 5
Ingland, Andrew, slave KER 2
Ingland, Fame, slave KER 2
Inglis, J. A., slave of CFD 2
Ingraham, W. P., slave of CHA 7-8
Ingraham, Wm. P., slaves of CHA 1
Ingram, Raney, slave KER 2
Innes, Catherine M. CHA 27
Irwin, R. W. LAN 4
Isaac, slave BAR 8
Isaac, slave BAR 7
Isaac, slave BAR 2
Isaac, slave GEO 7
Isaac, slave WIL 5
Isaac, slave COL 9
Isaac, slave ORA 1
Isaac, slave ORA 6
Isaac, slave NEW 9
Isaac, slave ORA 8
Isaac, slave SUM 2
Isaac, slave SUM 4
Isaac, slave SUM 6
Isaac, slave BEA 13
Isaac, slave BEA 11
Isaac, slave SPA 3
Isaac, slave of Esther C. Douglas CFD 1
Isaac, slave of WM. Mazyck CHA 11
Isaac, slave of L. Reid ABB 7
Isaac, slave of James Shumate AND 2
Isaac, slave of O. Towles EDG 7
Isabel, slave of Iverson J. Brock EDG 14
Isabel, slave of James Elis UNI 1
Isabel, slave of D. M. Rogers ABB 4
Isabella, slave SUM 10
Isabella, slave SUM 14
Isabella, slave ORA 8
Isabella, slave of W. B. Brooks ABB 11
Isabella, slave of Isaac A. Hilber EDG 2
Isabella, slave of A. P. Lacoste CFD 2
Isac, slave CHA 10
Isac, slave of WM. Ducass CHA 9
Isam, slave of R. Brady ABB 3
Isam, slave of F. W. Pickens EDG 9
Isham, slave SPA 4
Ishmael, slave MRN 2
Isom, slave of M. E. Hollingsworth EDG 12
Israel, slave BAR 12
Israel, slave SUM 7
Israel, slave COL 8
Isum, slave of W. Campbell ABB 12
Ivey, Gadi MBO 1
Ivy, Caroline SUM 2

Jaber, slave SUM 1
Jac, slave of John Rutledge BEA 2
Jack, slave BAR 4
Jack, slave BAR 14
Jack, slave BAR 10
Jack, slave CHA 12
Jack, slave GRE 3
Jack, slave ORA 2
Jack, slave FAI 8
Jack, slave DAR 4
Jack, slave SUM 8
Jack, slave SUM 8
Jack, slave SUM 5
Jack, slave SUM 6
Jack, slave SUM 9
Jack, slave UNI 7
Jack, slave DAR 4
Jack, slave DAR 3
Jack, slave DAR 2
Jack, slave DAR 2
Jack, slave SPA 1
Jack, slave WIL 6
Jack, slave HOR 2
Jack, slave MBO 4
Jack, slave COL 10
Jack, slave COL 8
Jack, slave of Archy(?) Adams LAU 1
Jack, slave of David Dickson PIC 6
Jack, slave of Natt Ellis BEA 2
Jack, slave of Sarah Hammond EDG 15
Jack, slave of Levi G. Holliway EDG 4
Jack, slave of Robt Jennings EDG 13
Jack, slave of J. Logan ABB 17
Jack, slave of A. Mazyck CHA 11

Jack, slave of
F. W. Pickens EDG 8
Jack, slave of
R. Timmerman EDG 5
Jack, slave of
J. L. Turnbull ABB 4
Jack, slave of
J. Venning CHA 7
Jackey, slave WIL 4
Jackson, slave BAR 13
Jackson, slave COL 10
Jackson, slave of
W. P. Brooks ABB 10
Jackson, David F., slave YRK 5
Jackson, E---
(free black) YRK 5
Jackson, John BAR 9
Jackson, John CHA 23
Jackson, John
(free black) BEA 14
Jackson, Martha, slave CHA 27
Jackson, Robert R YRK 4
Jackson, Stephen,
slave of CFD 3
Jackson, T.,
slave of ABB 6
Jacky, slave COL 1
Jacob, slave BAR 9
Jacob, slave BAR 8
Jacob, slave BAR 6
Jacob, slave COL 8
Jacob, slave GEO 1
Jacob, slave GEO 4
Jacob, slave GEO 6
Jacob, slave GEO 5
Jacob, slave GEO 8
Jacob, slave WIL 1
Jacob, slave SUM 10
Jacob, slave LAN 4
Jacob, slave FAI 6
Jacob, slave ORA 5
Jacob, slave NEW 8
Jacob, slave NEW 10
Jacob, slave of
T. Chatham ABB 11
Jacob, slave of
Sarah Gist UNI 2
Jacob, slave of
A. Harris ABB 18
Jacob, slave of
R. Robinson ABB 17
Jacobs, Charles,
slaves of LAU 4
Jake, slave DAR 3
Jake, slave of
J. Aiken ABB 7
Jake, slave of
Griffin Brazeal AND 2
Jake, slave of
Jordan Holliway EDG 12
Jake, slave of
Marshal ThompsonEDG 8
Jakes, Daniel BAR 10
James, mulatto BAR 1
James, slave CHA 10
James, slave UNI 5
James, slave LAN 2
James, slave NEW 1
James, slave NEW 4
James, slave NEW 5
James, slave NEW 7
James, slave SUM 5
James, slave SUM 10
James, slave SUM 11
James, slave COL 3
James, slave COL 3
James, slave COL 5
James, slave GEO 4
James, slave GEO 3
James, slave COL 10
James, slave of
Thos S. Bates EDG 18
James, slave of
George Bell EDG 18
James, slave of
M. W. Lyles EDG 13
James, slave of
Caleb Mitchell EDG 19
James, slave of
S. C. Sims UNI 1
James, slave of
R. Sites ABB 1
James, Hiram AND 2
James, John YRK 4
James, Rebecca HOR 2
James, William AND 3
James, William H. CHA 27
James,Wm GEO 2
Jamison, Wm PIC 2
Jane, slave CHA 12
Jane, slave BAR 3
Jane, slave COL 8
Jane, slave GEO 2
Jane, slave GEO 6
Jane, slave COL 6
Jane, slave MRN 2
Jane, slave DAR 4
Jane, slave SPA 1
Jane, slave SPA 3
Jane, slave SUM 5
Jane, slave SUM 8
Jane, slave SUM 10
Jane, slave LAN 5
Jane, slave LAN 2
Jane, slave GRE 1
Jane, slave GRE 5
Jane, slave UNI 4
Jane, slave SUM 12
Jane, slave NEW 9
Jane, slave NEW 1
Jane, slave FAI 2
Jane, slave FAI 1
Jane, slave ORA 6
Jane, slave ORA 1
Jane, slave ORA 4
Jane, slave ORA 3
Jane, slave ORA 2
Jane, slave of
Ephraim Andrews EDG 10
Jane, slave of
E. Carter ABB 15
Jane, slave of EDG 13
Thomas Chamberlain
Jane, slave of
J. Cochran ABB 15
Jane, slave of EDG 3
Joseph Cornshain
Jane, slave of
Elizabeth GarretEDG 1
Jane, slave of
David Harris EDG 5
Jane, slave of
E. Lott EDG 18
Jane, slave of
J. A. Mars ABB 4
Jane, slave of
J. P. Martin ABB 9
Jane, slave of
M. Mays ABB 18
Jane, slave of
Jas. H. Mims EDG 7
Jane, slave of
Owen Morgan EDG 13
Jane, slave of
H. Mosely ABB 18
Jane, slave of
F . Scaife UNI 1
Jane, slave of
W. Templeton ABB 17
Jane, slave of
John Terry EDG 4
Jane, slave of
E. Todd ABB 18
Jane, slave of
D. Wiley ABB 9
Jane, slave of
Stephen Wilson EDG 14
Janet, slave COL 7
Janet, slave MBO 3
January, slave SUM 4
January, slave FAI 7
January, slave BAR 8
January, slave BEA 13
January, slave CHA 5
Jasper, slave SUM 4
Javain, John A. CHA 24
Jef, slave of
A. J. Traylor EDG 10
Jefcoat, Barney BAR 6
Jefcoat, Benjamin LEX 3
Jeff, slave SUM 9
Jeff, slave of
R. Brady ABB 3
Jefferson, slave SUM 9
Jefferson, slave SUM 12
Jefferson, slave WIL 4
Jefferson, slave AND 3
of John A. Dacus
Jefford, Betsy,
slave CHA 20
Jeffrey, slave COL 1
Jeffreys, James P YRK 2
Jem, slave SPA 1
Jem, slave SPA 1
Jem, slave of
P. S. Brooks ABB 8
Jem, slave of
S. E. Edmonds ABB 2
Jem, slave of
J. Jorden ABB 5
Jem, slave of
W. Long Jr. ABB 14
Jem, slave of
E. Noble ABB 6
Jeme, slave of
T. W. Porcher CHA 3
Jemey, G. C.,
slave of CHA 6
Jemey, J.,
slave of CHA 6
Jemmy, slave COL 5
Jenings, John,
slaves of EDG 19
Jenkins, Dan,
slave BEA 8
Jenkins, Charles,
slave CHA 18
Jenkins, John CHA 18
Jenkins, Mary J. SUM 9
Jenkins, Perry BEA 14
Jennings, slave BAR 8
Jennings, John,
slave of UNI 1
Jennings, Joseph,
slave of EDG 4
Jennings, Robt,
slaves of EDG 13

Jennings, Tilmon, slave of EDG 18
Jenny, slave COL 12
Jenny, slave WIL 2
Jenny, slave WIL 5
Jenny, slave BAR 5
Jenny, slave BAR 7
Jenny, slave BEA 11
Jenny, slave GRE 4
Jenny, slave ORA 9
Jenny, slave of M. Jones ABB 1
Jenny, slave of Rebecca Simpson PIC 6
Jepson, Mary E. SUM 3
Jepson, Wm. SUM 1
Jeramy, slave SUM 13
Jere, slave MBO 2
Jerman, Edward D., slaves of CHA 9
Jerman, M., slaves of CHA 9
Jerry, slave COL 3
Jerry, slave LAN 3
Jerry, slave ORA 8
Jess, slave of George D. Anderson EDG 2
Jesse, slave UNI 5
Jesse, slave FAI 7
Jesse, slave NEW 3
Jesse, slave SUM 4
Jesse, slave MRN 1
Jesse, slave of J. W. Cooper EDG 7
Jesse, slave of J. C. Scott ABB 4
Jesse, slave of B. F. Mauldin AND 1
Jesse, slave of R. Woods ABB 14
Jessee, slave ORA 1
Jester, Abdel ABB 2
Jester, William ABB 12
Jerry, slave SPA 3
Jerry, slave DAR 1
Jet, slave of John Pervis CFD 2
Jeter, Jesse, slave of UNI 2
Jeter, L. C., slaves of UNI 2
Jeter, Matilda, slaves of UNI 1
Jevore, Elbert, slave of EDG 9
Jim, slave BEA 13
Jim, slave UNI 8
Jim, slave UNI 4
Jim, slave UNI 7
Jim, slave UNI 7
Jim, slave ORA 9
Jim, slave ORA 4
Jim, slave ORA 1
Jim, slave FAI 6
Jim, slave SUM 5
Jim, slave SUM 4
Jim, slave BAR 2
Jim, slave BAR 7
Jim, slave BAR 3
Jim, slave BAR 8
Jim, slave BAR 12
Jim, slave DAR 3
Jim, slave DAR 1
Jim, slave YRK 2
Jim, slave MBO 4
Jim, slave MRN 3
Jim, slave HOR 2
Jim, slave GEO 8
Jim, slave COL 3
Jim, slave COL 10
Jim, slave GEO 6
Jim, slave GEO 1
Jim, slave COL 11
Jim, slave COL 6
Jim, slave COL 7
Jim, slave COL 10
Jim, slave GEO 2
Jim, slave WIL 5
Jim, slave of John Adams EDG 1
Jim, slave of Eldred Bird EDG 12
Jim,slave of E. H. ChamberlanEDG 1
Jim, slave of T. Chatham ABB 11
Jim, slave of L. Cochran EDG 17
Jim, slave of Thos Furguson EDG 13
Jim, slave of B. Hollingsworth EDG 11
Jim, slave of L. C. Jeter UNI 2
Jim, slave of J. E. Padgett EDG 6
Jim, slave of J. Y. Partlow ABB 19
Jim, slave of Daniel Prescott EDG 1
Jim, slave of W. Thomas UNI 1
Jimmy, slave GEO 6
Jimmy, slave COL 8
Jimmy, slave GEO 8
Jimmy, slave of W. P. Ingraham CHA 8
Jin, slave of G. O. Wilkinson EDG 14
Jincey, slave YRK 3
Jincy, slave SUM 1
Jinney, slave of Wiley Glover EDG 14
Jincey, slave of J. C. Hays ABB 4
Jinney, slave of Alex Sharpton EDG 15
Jinnings, Boswell EDG 13
Jinny, slave WIL 3
Jinny, slave of J. Bausket EDG 5
Jno, slave COL 5
Jo, slave of H. C. Miller PIC 2
Jock, slave DAR 2
Joe, slave DAR 3
Joe, slave DAR 2
Joe, slave BAR 9
Joe, slave BAR 7
Joe, slave BAR 4
Joe, slave BAR 14
Joe, slave BAR 2
Joe, slave SUM 3
Joe, slave SUM 7
Joe, slave SUM 9
Joe, slave WIL 4
Joe, slave WIL 6
Joe, slave WIL 5
Joe, slave HOR 2
Joe, slave GEO 8
Joe, slave COL 10
Joe, slave COL 10
Joe, slave of John C. Allen EDG 6
Joe, slave of Keating Ball CHA 2
Joe, slave of Wosela Blalock EDG 9
Joe, slave of Dr. W. M. Burt EDG 11
Joe, slave of Lewis Carnes EDG 2
Joe, slave of Kennon Breazeal AND 3
Joe, slave of S. B. Brooks ABB 11
Joe, slave of J. A. Calhoun ABB 5
Joe, slave of John S.Carter EDG 7
Joe, slave of A. Giles ABB 8
Joe, slave of R. S. Holleman ABB 8
Joe, slave of B. HollingsworthEDG 11
Joe, slave of Amos Holmes EDG 3
Joe, slave of John B.Holmes EDG 6
Joe, slave of John Laurens CHA 1
Joe, slave of F. W. Pickens EDG 8
Joe, slave of Elisha RobertsonEDG 10
Joe, slave of Mrs. Rutledge CHA 11
Joe, slave of Benja. Skren(?) EDG 9
Joe, slave of R. Sproull ABB 18
Joe, slave of Dr. A. N. ToomerCHA 6
Joe, slave of Jane Turner EDG 9
Joe, slave of J. Venning CHA 7
Joel, slave COL 5
Joel, slave HOR 3
John, slave DAR 3
John, slave DAR 1
John, slave CHA 12
John, slave BAR 2
John, slave BAR 8
John, slave SUM 12
John, slave UNI 8
John, slave UNI 5
John, slave UNI 4
John, slave LAN 5
John, slave LAN 3
John, slave LAN 3
John, slave GRE 6
John, slave GRE 4
John, slave COL 12
John, slave COL 3
John, slave WIL 4
John, slave COL 10
John, slave COL 8
John, slave GEO 4
John, slave GEO 5
John, slave GEO 6
John, slave HOR 3
John, slave MRN 3
John, slave MRN 2
John, slave SUM 8
John, slave SUM 10
John, slave BEA 11
John, slave NEW 1
John, slave NEW 3
John, slave NEW 5

John, slave NEW 5
John, slave NEW 6
John, slave ORA 4
John, slave ORA 2
John, slave of W. Thorn FAI 8
John, slave FAI 7
John, slave of J. S. Chipley EDG 9
John, slave of Samuel Clarke EDG 2
John, slave of T. A. Conner ABB 16
John, slave of G. W. Cromer ABB 9
John, slave of W. J. Hanna CFD 1
John, slave of J. Harper ABB 13
John, slave of W. C. Haskell ABB 7
John, slave of Hollingsworth EDG 16
John, slave of Bennett Holtano EDG 20
John, slave of Edwd. D. Jerman CHA 9
John, slave of BEA 1 William C. Johnson
John, slave of Thomas G. Lamar EDG 14
John, slave of Allen McFarland CFD 1
John, slave of A. J. Rambo EDG 2
John, slave of EDG 13 J. C. Robertson
John, slave of W. Templeton ABB 17
John, slave of B. Whitesides CHA 6
John, slave of Sarah Wideman ABB 1
John, slave of ABB 6 Wilson & McGowan
Johnathan, slave of W. Tennant CHA 3
Johnny, slave FAI 2
Johnson, slave NEW 3
Johnson, slave of T. P. Mosely ABB 16
Johnson, A. S. GEO 1
Johnson, Affey (free black) CHA 27
Johnson, Alex BAR 6
Johnson, Anah, slave of FAI 4
Johnson, Andrew GRE 5
Johnson, Charles A CHA 17
Johnson, E. J. GEO 1
Johnson, Edward, slave of UNI 2
Johnson, Elizabeth MBO 3
Johnson, Frances, slave of CFD 1
Johnson,Green S. YRK 3
Johnson, H. ORA 3
Johnson, Harry, slave CHA 21
Johnson, Henrietta ABB 1
Johnson, Jas. H. CHR 5
Johnson, Jesse MBO 1
Joseph, Joseph, slave BEA 8
Johnson, Mary EDG 15
Johnson, Merion UNI 8
Johnson, Nancy BAR 10
Johnson, Capt. Nathan, slaves of BEA 1
Johnson, Peter, slave of AND 2
Johnson, Richard, slave CHA 18
Johnson, Robert ORA 6
Johnson, S., slave of ABB 13
Johnson, S. E. CHR 1
Johnson, Sally, slave BEA 8
Johnson, Samuel B WIL 4
Johnson, Sarah NEW 9
Johnson, Sibby, slave BEA 8
Johnson, Theodore CHA 26
Johnson, Wm BEA 10
Johnson, William, slave CHA 21
Johnson,William C., slave of BEA 1
Johnston, slave GEO 4
Johnston, George R. HOR 1
Johnston, Jane COL 6
Johnston, John (mulatto) COL 1
Johnston, Lucy (free black) KER 4
Johnston, S. A. LAN 4
Johnston, Wm HOR 1
Johny, slave COL 8
Joiner, slave BAR 4
Joiner, Flora BAR 3
Joiner, Robert, slave LEX 4
Jolly, Elizabeth HOR 3
Jolly, William AND 2
Jonas, slave GEO 7
Jones, Anney LAU 8
Jones, C., slave of EDG 11
Jones, Cornelia LAU 9
Jones, E., slaves of ABB 2
Jones, Francis, slave CHA 26
Jones, G. W. LAU 7
Jones, Hannah HOR 1
Jones, James Y. (mulatto) ABB 19
Jones, John E. COL 2
Jones, Levi, slave RIC 3
Jones, Lewis HOR 2
Jones, Lewis, slave of EDG 18
Jones, Moses ABB 1
Jones, M. ORA 5
Jones, M., slave of ABB 1
Jones, Martha CHR 1
Jones, Martha MBO 3
Jones, Martha LAU 6
Jones, Mary ORA 4
Jones, Meshack, slave RIC 3
Jones, Sarah ORA 4
Jones, Saml, slave RIC 3
Jones, Sarah B., slave of ABB 1
Jones, Susan J. ABB 14
Jones, Thomas AND 9
Jones, Thos, slave of EDG 5
Jones, Tobitha MBO 2
Jones, W. S., slave of ABB 12
Jor, slave DAR 4
Jor, slave DAR 3
Jordan, B., slaves of ABB 9
Jordan, E. DAR 4
Jordan, Martha HOR 1
Jordan, Mary Ann CFD 3
Jorden, J., slave of ABB 5
Jorden, Pamela A. ABB 9
Jose, Joseph, slave of AND 2
Joseph, slave BAR 2
Joseph, slave GRE 8
Joseph, slave GEO 5
Joseph, slave SPA 4
Joseph, slave COL 11
Joseph, slave COL 8
Joseph, slave WIL 4
Joseph, slave SUM 8
Joseph, slave ORA 9
Joseph,slave ORA 8
Joseph, slave NEW 10
Joseph, slave NEW 6
Joseph, slave of M. Hackett ABB 11
Josephine, slave COL 2
Josh, slave DAR 2
Joshua, slave COL 3
Joshua, slave of Jane Brooks EDG 19
Joshua, slave of K. Simmes Sr. CHA 1
Jourdan, Miss AND 6
Jowers, infant BAR 5
Jowers, William, slave of CFD 1
Joy, slave COL 3
Joyner, infant slave RIC 3
Juba, slave ORA 3
Juda, slave of Simon Briant AND 4
Juda, slave MBO 3
Juddy, slave COL 10
Judy, slave BAR 5
Judy, slave CHA 10
Judy, slave DAR 3
Jude, slave MRN 3
Jude, slave ORA 1
Jude, slave NEW 7
Judy, slave of W. B. Brooks ABB 11
Jude, slave of Alex Sharpton EDG 15
Judy, slave BEA 11
Judy, slave ORA 3
Judy, slave ORA 9
Judy, slave WIL 3
Judy, slave COL 8
Judy, slave WIL 5
Judy, slave COL 8
Judy, slave GEO 6
Judy, slave COL 2
Judy, slave GEO 1
Judy, slave COL 1
Judy, slave WIL 5
Judy, slave COL 12
Judy, slave COL 3
Juft, slave HOR 2
Juft, slave HOR 2
Jugnot,Antoinette CHA 6

Julia, slave SPA 3
Julia, slave WIL 1
Julia, slave COL 1
Julia, slave MRN 3
Julia, slave SUM 1
Julia, slave SUM 3
Julia, slave SUM 7
Julia, slave SUM 7
Julia, slave ORA 4
Julia, slave ORA 4
Julia, slave ORA 1
Julia, slave of Moses Holstun EDG 19
Julia, slave of Benja. Melton EDG 3
Julia Ann, slave SUM 3
Julian, slave of CHA 2 Henry L. Stevens
Juliana, slave YRK 4
Julianna, slave of A. P. Couner ABB 5
Juliet, slave BAR 4
Juliet, slave WIL 1
Julius (free black) YRK 1
Julius, slave of W. T. Frennan ABB 3
July, slave BAR 5
July, slave BAR 12
July, slave BAR 8
July, slave BEA 12
July, slave SUM 4
July, slave of John Tompkins EDG 17
June, slave COL 6
June, slave WIL 3
June, slave of BEA 1 Joseph M. Lawton
Junius, slave SPA 4
Juno, slave BAR 3
Juno, slave ORA 4
Juno, slave of CHA 2 Henry L. Stevens
Jupiter, slave of Saml Porcher CHA 12

Kaigler--see Keigler
Kaigler, DrucillaORA 9
Kate, slave BAR 3
Kate, slave CHA 5
Kate, slave of J. Fair ABB 15
Kate, slave of R. M. Fuller EDG 4
Kate, slave of CHA 3 Miss H. Gaillard
Kate, slave of A. Harris ABB 18
Katy, slave GRE 6
Katy, slave COL 3
Katy, slave COL 7
Katy, slave COL 8
Katy, slave of J. Watson ABB 10
Kay, F. L., slaves of ABB 15
Kay, Gabril AND 2
Kay, James G. ABB 8
Kay, Louisa E. AND 2
Keanor, slave of LAU 1 James Lewis
Keigler, George, slaves LEX 4
Keigler, Hariet, slaves LEX 4
Keith, J. DAR 1
Keith, Julia DAR 1
Kellar, John ORA 1
Kelley, Mary NEW 9
Kelly, Daniel AND 3
Kelly, Newton NEW 3
Kelly, William, slave of UNI 2
Kemerlin, Louisa ORA 1
Kemmerlin, B. F. ORA 1
Kemp, Margaret BAR 1
Kennady, William ORA 2
Kenneday, Alexander FAI 8
Kenneday, Jane, slave of FAI 8
Kennedy, Augustus L. ABB 14
Kennedy, Elizabeth ABB 2
Kennedy, George WIL 2
Kennedy, O., slave of FAI 1
Kennedy, Rachel WIL 2
Kennedy, Rebecca WIL 2
Kennedy, Robert CHA 6
Kennier, E. J. LAN 1
Kenny, M. EDG 11
Kenny, Robert, family of EDG 11
Kent, slave COL 10
Keown, James H. AND 5
Keown, Sarah E. AND 5
Kerby, Frances UNI 4
Kerny, Elizabeth CHR 4
Kesler, Henry SPA 4
Key, Ben KER 3
Key, Elizh. KER 3
Key, Elizabeth GRE 3
Key, James BAR 5
Key, Wm. KER 3
Keys, John AND 5
Keziah, slave of ABB 12 J. B. Clinkskale
Kibler, Andrew NEW 5
Kibler, Calvin NEW 10
Kichens, Elizabeth CHR 4
Kidd, Mary YRK 3
Kilgore, slave ofKER 2
Kilgore, J. S. KER 2
Kilgore, Mary SPA 1
Killin, Robt D., slaves of CFD 1
Kimbrell, Archy SPA 4
Kimbrel, Thomas YRK 1
Kinard, infant NEW 6
Kinard, Delilah BAR 1
Kinard, ElizabethNEW 8
Kinard, Martin H NEW 9
Kinard, Nicholas NEW 6
Kinerd, Michael LEX 3
King, Alex B GRE 1
King E. DAR 3
King, Eugenia AND 5
King, James, slaves of AND 2
King, Lavina E. LEX 1
King, Nancy CFD 1
King, Samuel HOR 3
King, Sarah J. COL 8
King, Thos B. COL 8
King, Thos W. HOR 1
King, Winny CFD 1
King, Wm., slaves of AND 8
Kirk, Gideon Ohead BEA 13
Kirkland, J. KER 2
Kirkland, Mary ORA 5
Kirkland, Milly, slave KER 2
Kirkland, R. A. BAR 12
Kirkmeyer, Otto CHA 24
Kirkpatrick, Thos S. CHR 5
Kirksey, Christopher PIC 2
Kirksey, Jamima, slave PIC 2
Kirkwood, Lemuel, slave CHA 19
Kitt, slave of M. J. Williams ABB 2
Kitt, slave of BEA 1 Dr. William C. Daniels
Kitty, slave of Keating Ball CHA 2
Kitty, slave of Dr. E. H. Deas CHA 3
Kitty, slave of H. E. Lucas CHA 7
Kiziah, slave of EDG 14 William T. Gardner
Kizzy, slave of Mary Harrison EDG 16
Klinck, Ann, slaveCHA 20
Klinck, Jane CHA 20
Knight, Franklin, slave of LAU 5
Knight, John, slaves of LAU 7
Knight, Jno COL 5
Knight, Mary CFD 3
Knight, William H.LAU 7
Knotts, William LEX 3
Knotts, William, slaves LEX 3
Knox, Nathaniel C PIC 6
Kornneck, Augustus CHA 25
Kugley, Hannah CHA 20
Kux(?), Elizth. SUM 3

LaBorde, Sarah, slave of EDG 8
Lacoste, A. P., slave of CFD 2
Ladd, Mrs., slaves of FAI 6
Lafar, Catharine CHA 24
Lafate, slave of M. Hackett ABB 11
Lafoucarde, J. B. CHA 26
Lake, Eligah NEW 1
Lake, Felix, family of EDG 6
Lake, Nathaniel H EDG 10
Lamar, Mary EDG 14
Lamar, Robt, slaves of EDG 14
Lamar, Thomas G., slaves of EDG 14
Lamar, William S. EDG 14
Lamb, Theodore UNI 8
Lambeth, Charlotte, slave of CFD 1
Lancaster, slave GRE 3
Lancaster, slave of T. W. Peyre CHA 4
Landers, Barnet GRE 5
Landon, slave YRK 1
Landry, Eliza CHA 18
Lane, Asenah NEW 2
Lang, E., slave of AND 3

Langston, James SUM 11
Langston, James G. AND 6
Langston, John AND 6
Lanham, Josias, slave of EDG 16
Lanhon, Jos., slave of FAI 8
Lanier, Bird AND 8
Lanier, Susan AND 7
Lard, Elizabeth BAR 3
Laroche, E., slave of CHA 6
Lassiter, Allen BAR 8
Latham, Cloa, slave PIC 1
Latham, Huldah, slave PIC 1
Latham, James PIC 1
Latham, Malissa, slave PIC 1
Latham, Rachael, slave PIC 1
Lathem, Cornelius AND 9
Latimer, Albert G. ABB 14
Latimer, J. M. Sr., slave of ABB 13
Latimer, S. A., slave of ABB 14
Latira, slave SUM 11
Latta, John B. YRK 4
Laura, slave BAR 12
Laura, slave SUM 6
Laura, slave SUM 11
Laura, slave FAI 2
Laura, slave COL 3
Laura, slave of C. Smith ABB 16
Laura, slave of J. S. Adams ABB 16
Laura, slave of Henry Rucker EDG 19
Laurence, slave SUM 6
Laurens, John, slave of CHA 1
Laurens, R., slaves of CHA 7
Lauson, slave SPA 3
Lavander, Lucy FAI 1
Lavenia, slave GEO 1
Lavenia, slave GEO 3
Lavenia, slave of Dr. Graves CHA 12
Lavinia, slave BAR 5
Lavinia, slave CHA 10
Lavinia, slave COL 9
Lavinia, slave COL 11
Lavinia, slave COL 1
Lavinia, slave MBO 2
Lavinia, slave GEO 6
Lavinia, slave of J. Allston ABB 6
Lavinia, slave of J. Bauskett EDG 5
Law, John BAR 8
Lawrence, slave BEA 12
Lawrence, slave ORA 2
Lawrence, slave of William Cose AND 1
Lawson, Sanford UNI 7
Lawson, Sarah UNI 6
Lawton, Joseph M., slaves of BEA 1
Lawton, Josiah ABB 3
Lawton, Margaret CHA 26
Lazarus, slave MBO 4
Lazarus, slave of M. Boulware FAI 1
Lazarus, June, slave CHA 19
League, Aurilla A GRE 2
Leah, slave BAR 7
Leah, slave SUM 13
Leah, slave SUM 9
Leah, slave COL 11
Leah, slave WIL 2
Leah, slave HOR 2
Leah, slave of M. B. Clark ABB 13
Leak, Jeremiah, slave of LAU 2
Leana(?), slave YRK 3
Leaphart, Catherine LEX 1
Leaphart, George LEX 1
Leaphart, George, slave LEX 1
Leaphart, Joseph, slave LEX 1
Leaphart, Michael, slave LEX 1
Leaphart, Samuel, slave LEX 1
Leathers, Joanna PIC 6
Leathersbee, Eldridge C. FAI 5
Ledbetter, H. W., slaves of ABB 16
Lee, slave of E. W. Perry EDG 3
Lee, Catharine ABB 8
Lee, John FAI 3
Lee, Mary PIC 1
Lee, R. DAR 4
Lee, S., slaves of ABB 4
Lee, Thomas PIC 5
Lee, Vicey BAR 6
Lee, W. DAR 4
Lee, William, slave of PIC 5
Legard, Elizabeth ABB 4
LeGard, Harriet P. E. ABB 4
Legare, Ann CHA 6
Legare, Dr. D., slave of CHA 6
Legare, John B. CHA 19
Legare, T. J., slave of CHA 6
Legget, Martha MBO 1
Legget, John CHA 23
Legg, William (free mulatto) CHA 26
Leister, Susan GRE 4
Lem, slave UNI 6
Lemmon, John J. SUM 12
Lemmons, James SPA 1
Lemmons, O. P. SPA 1
Lena, slave of H. E. Lucas CHA 7
Lembill(?), A., slave of FAI 5
Lennard, Bridget CHA 24
Lennard, Dennis CHA 24
Leonard, slave of H. H. Criswell ABB 17
Leonard, slave of V. Griffins Est. ABB 10
Leonora, slave SUM 6
Leonora, slave NEW 7
Leroy, Alice CHA 18
Lesette, slave COL 11
Leslie, slave MBO 3
Lesly, D., slaves of ABB 6
Lesly, Laminda D. ABB 8
Lesly, W., slave of ABB 7
Lesly, William J. ABB 8
Lester, slave BEA 12
Letecia, slave of Jas. Thomas UNI 1
Letha, slave of J. Martin ABB 8
Lettis, slave MRN 2
Letty, slave COL 3
Letty, slave COL 9
Letty, slave of B. Eakins ABB 9
Letty, slave of A. Harris ABB 18
Letty, slave of Jas. Lindsey ABB 14
Levenia, slave BEA 14
Levenia, slave WIL 5
Lever, Marcus L. M. NEW 8
Lever, Mary LEX 1
Levi, slave UNI 7
Levi, slave UNI 5
Levi, slave of Benjamin Cockrel FAI 1
Levina, slave SUM 9
Lewis, slave BAR 1
Lewis, slave BAR 6
Lewis, slave BEA 14
Lewis, slave SUM 6
Lewis, slave GRE 3
Lewis, slave GRE 2
Lewis, slave GEO 5
Lewis, slave NEW 2
Lewis, slave of Jas. F. Adams EDG 11
Lewis, slave of J. J. Barnet ABB 7
Lewis, slave of Margaret Cartlege EDG 16
Lewis, slave of Wm. Ducass CHA 9
Lewis, slave of G. W. Lomax ABB 16
Lewis, slave of Jas McComb ABB 6
Lewis, slave of D. New ABB 1
Lewis, slave of Dr. J. A. Palmer CHA 13
Lewis, slave of F. W. Pickens EDG 8
Lewis, slave of Seloin Stalmaker EDG 9
Lewis, slave of Elizabeth Sullivan EDG 15
Lewis, Artemas, slave of EDG 16
Lewis, Bell, slave PIC 1
Lewis, Ebenezer HOR 3
Lewis, Edward, slave CHA 22
Lewis, Elisha AND 3
Lewis, Harriet E. CHR 4
Lewis, Hiram PIC 2
Lewis, James, slaves of LAU 1
Lewis, James O., slave of PIC 5
Lewis, M. SPA 3
Lewis, Maria (free mulatto) CHA 27

Lewis, Nancy,
slave PIC 1
Lewis, Thos J. CHR 4
Lewis, W.,
slaves of FAI 2
Lezet, slave HOR 1
Lickie, Margaret CHA 19
Liddy, slave CHA 13
Liddy, slave YRK 3
Liemhouse, Margaret
CHA 24
Lifford, Eliza E. ABB 7
Lifford, J.,
slaves of ABB 7
Likey, slave BAR 1
Ligon, Daniel,
slave of LAU 6
Lilla, slave DAR 2
Lilla, slave DAR 4
Lilly, slave of
J. Bauskett EDG 5
Limas, slave NEW 8
Limehouse, Amos,
slave CHA 24
Limehouse, Margaret
CHA 24
Limehouse, William,
slave CHA 24
Limerick, slave GRE 5
Linch, A. W.,
slave of ABB 7
Linda, slave COL 7
Linda, slave GEO 2
Linda, slave COL 1
Linda, slave of
J. Brownlee ABB 8
Linda, slave of
B. Jordan ABB 9
Linda, slave of
F. B. Logan ABB 9
Linda, slave of
J. Mobley FAI 3
Linder, Mary COL 2
Lindsay, Jas.,
slave of ABB 14
Lindy, slave of
Stanmore Watson EDG 18
Lining, Edward B. CHA 16
Link, J.,
slave of ABB 5
Linson, W. CHA 13
Linus, slave COL 6
Lipscomb, John,
family of EDG 11
Lipscombe, Jemima ABB 18
Lipscombe, T. P.,
slaves of ABB 18
Lisbon, slave COL 11
Little, Henry CFD 2
Little, Jonas UNI 6
Little, Mary J. S. LAU 5
Little, Robert, LAU 2
slave of
Liverett, Martha AND 5
Livingston, Henry ORA 2
Livingston, Marshall NEW 10
Liz, slave BAR 6
Lizzie, slave SUM 14
Lizzie, slave of
Uriah Inabnit EDG 18
Lizzy, slave CHA 10
Lizzy, slave of
J. A. Calhoun ABB 5
Lizzy, slave of
A. P. Pool ABB 18
Lloyd, Porcher CHA 15
Loadholt, Charles BEA 14
Loadholt, Martin BEA 14
Lockhart, Emma(?) SPA 1
Lockhart, J.,
slave of ABB 13
Lockhart, Joseph KER 3
Logan, A.,
slave of ABB 11
Logan, A. J.,
slave of ABB 9
Logan, Andrew ABB 11
Logan, Andrew J. ABB 9
Logan, Charles B EDG 13
Logan, F. B.,
slave of ABB 9
Logan, J.,
slave of ABB 17
Logan, J.,
slave of ABB 9
Logan, Jane EDG 13
Logan, Susan EDG 13
Lomax, Eliza ABB 13
Lomax, G. W.,
slaves of ABB 16
Lomax, L. H.,
slave of ABB 6
Lomax, Mary ABB 12
London, slave GEO 5
London, slave SUM 7
London, slave of
N. L. Toomer CHA 6
Long, Elizabeth MBO 1
Long, Francis E. NEW 4
Long, James,
slave of LAU 2
Long, John MRN 1
Long, John A. NEW 8
Long, Joseph,
slave of EDG 20
Long, Josephus
C. NEW 4
Long, Mary CHR 3
Lonn, slave of
Joseph Rearden EDG 12
Lopez, Moses CHA
Lorick, George,
slave LEX 1
Lorick, George,
slaves LEX 2
Lot, slave DAR 2
Lothy, slave MBO 3
Lott, E.,
slaves of EDG 18
Louis, slave UNI 4
Louis, slave LAN 2
Louis, slave of
Dr. W. M. Burt EDG 11
Louisa, slave GRE 3
Louisa, slave UNI 4
Louisa, slave SUM 10
Louisa, slave BEA 11
Louisa, slave WIL 5
Louisa, slave MBO 2
Louisa, slave MBO 1
Louisa, slave NEW 9
Louisa, slave NEW 10
Louisa, slave FAI 1
Louisa, slave of
G. W. Duvall CFD 2
Louisa, slave of
M. A. Morris EDG 9
Louisa, slave of
Ellen L. Parker ABB 5
Louisa, slave of
W. C. Scott ABB 3
Louisa, slave of
W. Smith ABB 9
Louisa, slave of
W. Templeton ABB 17
Louisa, slave of
T. Thompson ABB 5
Louise, slave NEW 3
Louisina, slave of
D. Harris EDG 5
Louiza, slave SUM 6
Louiza, slave LAU 1
Louiza, slave EDG 16
Loura, slave of
W. R. Smith LAU 1
Love, Rebecca,
slave of AND 3
Love Berry, slave
of Z. Harris EDG 4
Lovegreen, A. A. CHA 26
Loveless, Susan,
slave of EDG 3
Loveless, Thos H. EDG 3
Lovell, Eliza V. WIL 3
Low, Mary C. AND 2
Low, Sarah ABB 14
Low, William J. ABB 14
Lowerman, John,
slave LEX 3
Lowery(?), Conrad,
slave of EDG 6
Lowndes, Phillis,
slave CHA 17
Lowndes, R.,
slave of CHA 10
Lownence, R. G.,
slaves of AND 7
Loyd, slave GEO 4
Lucas, Daniel CFD 2
Lucas, Eliza Ann
(free mulatto) CHA 25
Lucas, Est.,
slaves of CHA 7
Lucas, H. E.,
slaves of CHA 7
Lucas, William,
slaves of CHA 10
Lucinda, slave LAN 2
Lucinda, slave LAN 2
Lucinda, slave WIL 1
Lucinda, slave NEW 4
Lucinda, slave FAI 8
Lucinda, slave NEW 3
Lucinda, slave NEW 1
Lucinda, slave of
Archy Adams LAU 1
Lucinda, slave of
Yancey Freeman EDG 13
Lucinda, slave of
Conrad Lowery(?) EDG 6
Lucius, Nancy EDG 13
Luck, slave BAR 7
Luck, slave of
Langdon Chevis BEA 2
Luck, Elizabeth SPA 1
Lucretia, slave COL 2
Lucretia, slave COL 7
Lucretia, slave NEW 7
Lucy, slave BAR 8
Lucy, slave COL 2
Lucy, slave GEO 1
Lucy, slave COL 10
Lucy, slave GEO 6
Lucy, slave CHA 12
Lucy, slave MBO 3
Lucy, slave DAR 3
Lucy, slave NEW 6
Lucy, slave SPA 3
Lucy, slave WIL 1
Lucy, slave ORA 9

Lucy, slave ORA 1
Lucy, slave FAI 1
Lucy, slave BEA 13
Lucy, slave BEA 12
Lucy, slave SUM 14
Lucy, slave SUM 5
Lucy, slave SUM 3
Lucy, slave GRE 8
Lucy, slave GRE 1
Lucy, slave of Wm. Bouknight EDG 19
Lucy, slave of Elias Earle PIC 5
Lucy, slave of William Forrester BEA 1
Lucy, slave of F. Martin ABB 2
Lucy, slave of Thos Porcher Est. CHA 3
Lucy, slave of Henry Spires EDG 2
Lucy, slave of R. M. Talbert EDG 1
Lucy, slave of O. Towles EDG 7
Lucy, slave of J. Watson ABB 10
Luke, slave MBO 3
Luke, slave of F. W. Pickens EDG 8
Lunar, Wm. CHA 9
Lunday, A., family of EDG 6
Luny, slave of J. A. Norwood ABB 5
Lydia, slave BAR 7
Lydia, slave BAR 11
Lydia, slave BAR 14
Lydia, slave GEO 2
Lydia, slave GRE 6
Lydia, slave UNI 8
Lydia, slave of J. Bausket EDG 5
Lydia, slave of Wm. Moss EDG 11
Lydia, slave of John T. Simpson EDG 10
Lykes, Cumptia, slave RIC 1
Lykes, Riban, slave RIC 1
Lyles, John J. EDG 13
Lyles, M. W., slave of EDG 13
Lymbrick, slave SUM 14
Lyon, Joseph ABB 6
Lynn, Joshua CHR 1
Lyon, Priscilla FAI 6
Lyon, Samuel ABB 6
Lyons, John, slave of EDG 11
Lysot, slave GEO 5

McAllister, N., slave of AND 5
McAndrew, Patrick CHA 16
McAteer, Jos. F. LAN 2
McBride, Ann ABB 2
McBride, Mary ABB 2
McBride, R., slave of FAI 6
McBride, Saml SUM 12
McCain, Elizabeth EDG 12
McCall, Dougal MRN 3
McCall, Duncan CFD 1
McCallister, Saml WIL 2
McCallum, E. J. MBO 1
McCammon, B. CHR 2
McCammon, Calphurna CHR 2
McCants, slave NEW 5
McCants, David J ABB 18
McCants, Joseph J. WIL 2
McCants, W., slave of CHA 6
McCarter, Menor YRK 5
McCartney, J., Est., slave of ABB 2
McCartney, John ABB 2
McCarty, J., slave of EDG 18
McCaslain, RobertABB 4
McCaslan, Robert ABB 2
McCatherin, Thadeus CHR 3
McCaw, W. H., slave of ABB 13
McCelvey, Jas. M., slave of ABB 3
McClain, Bryant WIL 3
McClam(?), Eleanor WIL 2
McClary, Sidney V. WIL 5
McClellan, A., slaves of CHA 9
McClure, Sarah A CHA 19
McClurge, Jane GRE 6
McClurge, Margaret GRE 6
McColl, Daniel MBO 1
McColl, Duncan MBO 1
McColl, John, slaves of LAU 8
McCollum, John A MBO 2
McCollough, Sitgreave P. YRK 2
McCollough, Rebecca YRK 2
McColman, Isabella CFD 2
McColough, Elizabeth YRK 4
McComb, Jas., slave of ABB 6
McConnel, Aud., slave of FAI 5
McCord, Nancy ABB 12
McCormick, William CHA 27
McCoy, Jesse KER 3
McCrary, Jane ABB 7
McCraw, Sarah SPA 1
McCray, E. ORA 1
McCreight, RobertYRK 3
McCrorey, J. T., slave of FAI 8
McCrorey, James, slave of FAI 8
McCrorey, Mary T FAI 8
McCrory, John, slave of FAI 4
McCullough, BenjaminSPA 1
McCullough, D., slave of FAI 8
McCullough, James UNI 4
McCullough, William H. EDG 10
McCully, J., slave of FAI 1
McDaniel, Archy GRE 2
McDaniel, BenjaminGRE 3
McDaniel, J., slaves of LAU 6
McDaniel, Maryan EDG 1
McDill, John CHR 1
McDill, John, slaves of CHR 1
McDonald, John SUM 11
McDonald, Sarah DAR 2
McDowell, Nancy Jane HOR 1
McDowell, Tho HOR 1
McDuffie, slaves of ABB 13
McDuffie, Aldr MRN 3
Macelhaney, Leonora COL 5
McElrath, children(?) SPA 4
McElrath, M. SPA 4
McElvane, Rebecca B. SUM 11
McFadden, Mary N. SUM 12
McFadden, Rebecca D. WIL 3
McFaddin, Elias SUM 11
McFail, James BEA 12
McFail, John BAR 11
McFall, John, slaves of AND 6
McFarland, Allen, slaves of CFD 1
McFarland, John D.CFD 1
McGarrity, J. H. CHR 2
McGaw, Mary E. ABB 5
McGee, B., slaves of AND 1
McGentry, Mary CHA 21
McGill, Catherine AND 5
McGill, Mary Ann WIL 4
McGowen, Robert LAU 1
McGowen, Wm., slaves of LAU 2
McGown, Janus CHA 23
McGuin, Alexander CHA 15
McHannahan, William CHA 27
McIlwain, Eliza ABB 15
McIlwain, Jane ABB 15
McIlwain, Samuel ABB 15
McInnis, Daniel MRN 3
McJunkin, Joseph UNI 1
McKain, Elizh. KER 4
McKain, J. R. KER 4
McKain, Sarah KER 4
McKay, Thomas B. CHA 24
McKee, Henry BEA 10
Mackee, Mary BEA 10
McKee, Milly, slave BEA 8
McKellar, Archd MRN 3
McKeller, Alexdr MRN 3
McKensie, Elisha GRE 1
McKenzie, Frances CHA 16
McKenzie, James CHA 16
McKeown, Mary UNI 5
McKewn, John ABB 12
Mackie, Amanda CHA 21
McKie, George, slave of EDG 15
Mackie, Narcissas CHA 22
McKie, Thomas, slaves of EDG 15
McKinney, Ann PIC 1
McKinney, John PIC 2
McKinney, Sarah PIC 2
McKinney, Thos PIC 2

McKinny, Elizabeth R. AND 6
McKleduff, James FAI 6
McLain, Sarah ABB 5
McLaurin, Catharine MBO 1
McLelland, infant slave RIC 3
McLeod, Catharine MBO 3
M'Lemor, Nancy BAR 6
McLeod, Vernon SUM 11
McLoud, A. F. CHA 5
McMahan, Sarah C. AND 5
McMahan, Susan AND 3
McMahan, W. GRE 6
McManus, Goody EDG 3
McManus, James LAN 3
McManus, Rosanna CFD 3
McMessin, slave of FAI 4
McMillan, Richard BAR 1
McMillen, Alex GRE 4
McMillen, Ben, slave CFD 2
McMurry, James W. AND 3
McMurry, M. N. LAN 2
McNamarra, Lawrence CHA 21
McNeal, John, slave of FAI 4
McNeill, Martha MRN 1
McNelly, Malinda GRE 1
McNie, Alexander CHA 23
McNeese, J. DAR 3
McNinch, John CHR 3
McNinch, Joseph CHR 3
McNinch, S. N. CHR 3
McQuage, John CFD 2
McQueen, Alexander, slaves of CFD 1
McQueen, D. M. HOR 2
McRa, J. S., slaves of KER 5
McRae, Andrew MBO 3
McRae, Isabella MBO 1
McRae, Jacob, slave KER 3
McRae, Roderic MBO 4
McSwain(?), Charles KER 3
McWhorter, Mary PIC 6
McWilliams, DanielWIL 6

Mack, slave CHA 5
Mack, slave of O. Towles EDG 7
Maco, slave SPA 3
Madden, Frances, slave of LAU 8
Madden, Mabree, slaves of LAU 7
Maddox, R., slave of ABB 12
Madison, slave of A. J. Traylor EDG 10
Magill, James W. ABB 2
Magill, John T. ABB 12
Mahala, slave MRN 2
Mahala, slave UNI 8
Mahala, slave of L. H. Lomax ABB 6
Mahaly, slave of W. B. Brooks ABB 11
Mahaly, slave of Sicily Hobson UNI 1
Mahoney, CatharineCHA 17
Mahoney, Jemmy CHA 17
Mahony, CatharineCHA 16
Mahony, Jane CHA 16
Major, slave GRE 1
Major, slave ORA 8
Major, slave SPA 3
Major, slave YRK 4
Malcom, John CHA 19
Maler, slave MRN 2
Malinda, slave SPA 4
Malinda, slave GRE 4
Malinda, slave SUM 6
Mall, slave GEO 1
Mallett, Harriet SUM 13
Malloy, Mary A. CFD 2
Malone, Daniel UNI 7
Malone, Sarah UNI 7
Maloney, Nelly CHA 16
Malony, Briget CHA 16
Malony, Sampson CHA 16
Manda, slave of Daniel Ouzts EDG 5
Mandey, slave of D. McCullough FAI 8
Maner, John S., slaves of BEA 2
Mangum, Elisha CFD 3
Mangum, Jacob, slave of CFD 3
Manigault, C., slaves of CHA 7
Manker, Rebecca BEA 14
Mann, M. S., slave of ABB 6
Manning, ElizabethPIC 2
Mansfield, Tom, slave CHA 25
Manton, slave WIL 6
Maples, Thos Jr SUM 9
Mapus, PrissillerLEX 3
March, slave GEO 3
March, slave COL 1
March, slave WIL 5
March, slave SUM 8
March, slave ORA 7
March, slave of EDG 10 William Culbreath
March, slave of Capt. Robertson CHA 2
March, slave of Dr. M. Waring CHA 2
Marcina, slave UNI 3
Marcus, slave MBO 3
Marcus, slave NEW 5
Marcy, slave GEO 2
Margaret, slave SUM 2
Margaret, slave SUM 2
Margaret, slave SUM 4
Margaret, slave NEW 6
Margaret, slave FAI 2
Margaret, slave ORA 9
Margaret, slave ORA 5
Margaret, slave COL 9
Margaret, slave COL 5
Margaret, slave COL 12
Margaret, slave GRE 8
Margaret, slave BAR 2
Margaret, slave of Benj. F. Buckner BEA 2
Margaret, slave of Mary Bush EDG 3
Margaret, slave of Z. Harris EDG 4
Margaret, slave of Jos. Lanhon FAI 8
Margaret, slave of J. A. Norwood ABB 5
Margaret, slave of Thos L. Shans EDG 16
Margarett, slave LAN 2
Margt(?), slave BAR 13
Maria, slave BAR 13
Maria, slave BAR 12
Maria, slave BAR 11
Maria, slave ORA 8
Maria, slave FAI 7
Maria, slave COL 11
Maria, slave COL 9
Maria, slave COL 10
Maria, slave COL 2
Maria,slave UNI 4
Maria, slave UNI 6
Maria, slave GEO 7
Maria, slave of R. W. Coleman FAI 3
Maria, slave of John DangerfieldCHA 1
Maria, slave of WM. Daniel EDG 18
Maria, slave of Wm. Ducass CHA 9
Maria, slave of J. Herrin EDG 18
Maria, slave of F. L. Kay ABB 15
Maria, slave of M. Moore ABB 13
Mariah, slave SUM 5
Mariah, slave SUM 9
Mariah, slave SUM 11
Mariah, slave SUM 7
Mariah, slave SUM 13
Mariah, slave SUM 3
Mariah, slave GEO 6
Mariah, slave LAN 4
Mariah, slave EDG 15
Mariah, slave of Z. W. Carwile EDG 7
Marianna, slave COL 9
Marilla, slave ORA 8
Marinda, slave of B. Sale ABB 10
Marinda, slave of W. Templeton ABB 17
Marion, slave UNI 8
Marion, slave of J. Lockhart ABB 13
Marion, B. B., slave of CHA 13
Maritha, slave ORA 8
Mark, slave of D. Rudd ABB 19
Mark, slave of Tabitha Tillman EDG 16
Markley, Anna GRE 1
Marmaduke, slave COL 1
Mars, J. A., slaves of ABB 4
Marshal, slave GRE 6
Marshal, slave SUM 1
Marshall, A. KER 3
Marshall, Andrew, slave CHA 21
Marshall, Isabella ABB 10
Marshall, J. F., slave of ABB 6
Marshall, John LAN 4
Marshall, Mary KER 3
Marshall, S., slaves of ABB 10
Marshall, S. L., slave of ABB 10
Marshall, T. C. CHA 21
Marth, slave WIL 2

Martha, slave BAR 1
Martha, slave UNI 8
Martha, slave UNI 8
Martha, slave COL 10
Martha, slave ORA 9
Martha, slave FAI 7
Martha, slave NEW 10
Martha, slave NEW 6
Martha, slave NEW 8
Martha, slave of W. Black ABB 7
Martha, slave of Walter Brice FAI 3
Martha, slave of S. V. Cain ABB 18
Martha, slave of A. Hunter ABB 8
Martha, slave of Henry May EDG 8
Martha, slave of S. J. Mobley FAI 6
Martha, slave of CHA 13 Dr. J. S. Palmer
Martha, slave of Martha Powe CFD 2
Martha, slave of J. W. Ritchey ABB 14
Martha, slave of M. Ritchey ABB 12
Martha, slave of J. A. StevensonUNI 2
Martha, slave of W. Tennant CHA 3
Martha, slave of J. Watson ABB 10
Martin, slave SUM 7
Martin, slave ORA 4
Martin, slave of Benjn Hatcher EDG 16
Martin, children BAR 6
Martin,A., slave of ABB 7
Martin, Eliza H. ABB 7
Martin, Elizabeth S. ABB 4
Martin, F., slave of ABB 2
Martin, J., slaves of ABB 8
Martin, J. A., slave of ABB 8
Martin, J. A., slaves of FAI 4
Martin, J. P., slave of ABB 9
Martin, James AND 5
Martin, James Sr ABB 4
Martin, John E. AND 2
Martin ,Lavinia A ABB 2
Martin, Lewis, slave of LAU 6
Martin, M. C. AND 7
Martin, Mary E. ABB 17
Martin, Mary E. FAI 4
Martin, Nancy ABB 3
Martin, Nancy PIC 6
Martin, Phil ORA 2
Martin, Wm., slaves of AND 3
Mary, slave BAR 12
Mary, slave BAR 13
Mary, slave BAR 8
Mary, slave CHA 13
Mary, slave ORA 9
Mary, slave NEW 8
Mary, slave NEW 9
Mary, slave NEW 6
Mary, slave NEW 2
Mary, slave NEW 1
Mary, slave ORA 9
Mary, slave ORA 7
Mary, slave ORA 3
Mary, slave ORA 2
Mary, slave SUM 1
Mary, slave SUM 3
Mary, slave SUM 4
Mary, slave SUM 5
Mary, slave SUM 8
Mary, slave MRN 2
Mary, slave MRN 2
Mary, slave GEO 5
Mary, slave GEO 6
Mary, slave GEO 1
Mary, slave GEO 4
Mary, slave GEO 2
Mary, slave COL 1
Mary, slave COL 7
Mary, slave WIL 5
Mary, slave COL 11
Mary, slave COL 9
Mary, slave BEA 13
Mary, slave BEA 11
Mary, slave UNI 7
Mary, slave UNI 6
Mary, slave UNI 5
Mary, slave LAN 1
Mary, slave GRE 6
Mary, slave GRE 1
Mary, slave GRE 4
Mary, slave of J. C. Brice FAI 1
Mary, slave of Wm. Brown EDG 13
Mary, slave of A. M. Cox ABB 2
Mary, slave of Ellen Dozier EDG 20
Mary, slave of Wm Ducass CHA 9
Mary, slave of S. T. Gourdin CHA 13
Mary, slave of J. G. Hammond EDG 15
Mary, slave of A. N. Hindman FAI 8
Mary, slave of Wade Holsten EDG 18
Mary, slave of J. H. Hughes EDG 6
Mary, slave of J. Hughey ABB 9
Mary, slave of Lewis Jones EDG 18
Mary, slave of James King AND 2
Mary, slave of E. Lang AND 3
Mary, slave of William Lee PIC 5
Mary, slave of J. Lifford ABB 7
Mary, slave of T. W. Porcher CHA 3
Mary, slave of J. W. Prother ABB 3
Mary, slave of N. Shirleys Est ABB 14
Mary, slave of R. Smith UNI 2
Mary, slave of John Thurman EDG 14
Mary, slave of J. Vance ABB 17
Mary, slave of Z. Walker EDG 4
Mary, slave of Mabitha Watson EDG 3
Mary, slave of E. C. West EDG 2
Mary, slave of EDG 17 William J. Wightman
Mary, slave of J. L. Youngue FAI 3
Maryan, slave of Jas. S. GuignardEDG 4
Maryann, slave COL 9
Mary A., slave NEW 10
Mary Ann, slave ORA 8
Mary Ann, slave SUM 8
Mary Ann, slave BEA 12
Mary Ann, slave of Natt Ellis BEA 2
Mary Ann, slave of T. OConner EDG 6
Mason, John, slave LAU 4
Mason, Ransom SPA 4
Mason, William CHA 26
Massey, Sion, slave of AND 5
Masten, Reuben GRE 3
Masters, Amanda PIC 5
Masters, Caroline PIC 5
Masters, John H. PIC 5
Masters, Washington PIC 5
Mat, slave UNI 7
Mat, slave of H. Mays ABB 15
Mathew, slave GRE 5
Mathews, John CHA 27
Mathews, Lewis ABB 5
Mathias, slave of R. Laurens CHA 7
Mathis, Elliot P. NEW 8
Matilda, slave SUM 11
Matilda, slave of F. W. Pickens EDG 8
Matilda, slave of Jos. A. Talbert EDG 17
Mation, slave GEO 5
Matteson, B. F., mulatto AND 1
Matthews, slave of Moses Chamblee AND 2
Matthew, slave of Wm. Homes AND 2
Matthews, slave COL 3
Matthews, slave of FAI 2
Matthews, Elizabeth EDG 5
Matthews, Emeline EDG 19
Matthews, Hester LAU 7
Matthews, Isaac CHA 17
Matthews, Simeon, family of EDG 5
Matthis, Caleb EDG 8
Mattison, E., slave of ABB 14
Mattison, James AND 1
Mattison, Reece AND 1
Mattison, Wm., slave of AND 1
Mattison, William H. ABB 14
Maul, slave COL 12
Maul, slave HOR 2
Maull, David, slave of EDG 3
Mauson, slave SUM 6
Maxcy, Sophia ORA 6

Maxwell, John,
slave of PIC 5
Maxwell, R. A.,
slave of AND 7
Maxwell, Samuel,
slave of PIC 5
May, slave GEO 1
May, slave BAR 3
May, slave of
J. Bausket EDG 5
May, Henry,
slave of EDG 8
May, Henry Clay EDG 5
May, Martha COL 5
May, Olivetta COL 5
Maybin, Benjamin NEW 10
Mayer, John, slave LEX 2
Mayes, Joseph UNI 6
Mayfield, Abram AND 6
Mayfield, Green B. CHR 5
Mayfield, White AND 6
Maynad, Mary,
slaves of EDG 10
Mayo, Isadora,
slave RIC 1
Mays, George W. BAR 3
Mays, H.,
slave of ABB 16
Mays, James EDG 8
Mays, John J. EDG 6
Mays, M., slaves of ABB 18
Mays, Medy ABB 17
Mays, S., family of EDG 6
Mayson, G. C.,
slave of EDG 4
Mazyck, A.,
slaves of CHA 11
Mazyck, Peter CHA 18
Mazyck, Wm.,
slaves of CHA 11
Meadors, Julia SPA 1
Mealing, Ella L. EDG 15
Means, Friday,
slave BEA 8
Means, Jacob,
slave BEA 9
Means, Joshua BEA 9
Means, Mary,
slave BEA 8
Means, Sibby,
slave BEA 8
Means, Tyra,
slave BEA 9
Means, W.,
slaves of ABB 7
Meetts, John LEX 2
Mellard, Rachel COL 5
Melton, Benja.,
slave of EDG 3
Melton, Lewis,
slave of CFD 1
Melvina, slave UNI 8
Melvina, slave HOR 1
Melvina, slave of
M. C. Tallman ABB 4
Mely, slave of
S. Marshall ABB 10
Memory, free black SPA 3
Menda, slave COL 12
Meredith, A.,
slaves of AND 8
Meriman, slave GEO 8
Metta, slave MRN 1
Michau, Hester WIL 4
Michel, Katharine AND 4
Mickle, Jonathan,
slaves of FAI 8
Mickler, Edward BEA 12
Micus(?), Martin EDG 13
Middleton, Caroline EDG 15
Middleton, Estate
H., slaves of BEA 14
Middleton, John F.,
slaves of EDG 15
Middleton, Phoeby CHA 15
Mike, slave of
Matilda Jeter UNI 1
Milam, John,
slave LAU 6
Miledge, slave of
Tilmon Jennings EDG 18
Miles, slave YRK 2
Miles, slave of
Lewis Melton CFD 1
Miles, A.,
slave of EDG 18
Miles, Jas SUM 11
Miles, Sally,
slaves of EDG 3
Mileus(?), slave YRK 3
Miley, slave BEA 12
Milford, Ede T. B. ABB 14
Milleage, slave BAR 12
Millen, Jane CHR 4
Millen, Joseph E. CHR 4
Miller, slave SUM 6
Miller, A. T.,
slave of ABB 15
Miller, Albert LAU 4
Miller, Claudia COL 1
Miller, E. S. SPA 4
Miller, H. C.,
slaves of PIC 2
Miller, James,
slave RIC 3
Miller, James CHA 18
Miller, John,
slave of EDG 2
Miller, John,
slave of AND 7
Miller, John C.,
slave of AND 7
Miller, Margaret
A. ABB 15
Miller, Sarah A. KER 2
Miller, Sarah E. PIC 4
Milley, slave SUM 2
Milley, slave NEW 2
Milley, slave GEO 6
Milley, slave COL 9
Millhouse, Henrietta
BAR 3
Millson, slave of
Joel Cose AND 1
Millwood, Sunsberry
UNI 4
Milly, slave BAR 3
Milly, slave BAR 11
Milly, slave NEW 1
Milly, slave ORA 4
Milly, slave LAN 1
Milly, slave of
S. Brice FAI 3
Milly, slave of
J. W. Cobb ABB 15
Milly, slave of
D. Lesly ABB 6
Milly, slave of
T. E. Powe CFD 2
Milly, slave of
Thos K. Robeson CFD 1
Milly, slave of
C. Ruffs Est. ABB 15
Milly, slave of
A. Vance ABB 11
Milne, Anne,
slave BEA 8
Milne, Betsy,
slave BEA 8
Milne, Plymouth,
slave BEA 8
Milne, William,
slave BEA 8
Milus(?), slave YRK 3
Mima, slave UNI 6
Mima, slave of
W. C. Calhoun ABB 19
Mima, slave of
H. C. Hurlong EDG 2
Mime, slave of
S. Marshall ABB 10
Mims, F., family
of EDG 11
Mims, James BAR 6
Mims, Jas. H.,
slave of EDG 7
Mims, Lewis,
family of EDG 12
Mina, slave of
F. W. Pickens EDG 9
Minda, slave SUM 1
Minda, slave WIL 1
Minerva, slave UNI 8
Minerva, slave UNI 7
Minerva, slave UNI 4
Minerva, slave LAN 2
Minerva, slave of
Edward Emory PIC 6
Minerva, slave of
F. W. Pickens EDG 8
Mingo, slave FAI 3
Mingo, slave WIL 4
Mingo, slave CHA 13
Mingo, slave of
H. M. Prince ABB 7
Minna, slave ORA 3
Minnick, John S. NEW 6
Minos, slave ORA 4
Minta, slave MRN 3
Minta, slave of
Hugh Mosley EDG 10
Mintey, slave YRK 3
Minty, slave BEA 12
Minty, slave COL 10
Minty, slave of
W. Young ABB 13
Minus, slave of
Mr. Colburn CHA 9
Miott, Ester
(free mulatto) CHA 23
Miott, Harriet CHA 22
Mira, slave RIC 2
Mirick, slave ORA 4
Mise, Joshua UNI 7
Mitcheal, Caroline
S. LAU 7
Mitcheal, Francis LAU 7
Mitchel, Ann,
slave CHA 19
Mitchel, Jacob,
slave CHA 19
Mitchell, infant EDG 12
Mitchell, Caleb EDG 19
Mitchell, Dempsy BAR 6
Mitchell, John C. EDG 19
Mitchell, John T.,
slave of EDG 19
Mitchell, Martha EDG 12
Mitchell, Mary A. EDG 19
Mitchell, Thos E. EDG 19

Mitchell, Treasy EDG 12
Mitchell, Wm. C. EDG 18
Mitchem, Wm PIC 4
Mitchum, Ambrose WIL 1
Mitty, slave of W. Brezeal AND 2
Mixon, Mary BAR 2
Mobley, slave of FAI 1
Mobley, Albert W. EDG 18
Mobley, D., slaves of FAI 8
Mobley, D., slaves of FAI 8
Mobley, J., slave of FAI 3
Mobley, James B., slaves of FAI 6
Mobley, S. J., slave of FAI 6
Mobley, Thomas FAI 6
Mobley, William, family of EDG 5
Mobley, William M. FAI 6
Moggy, slave DAR 2
Molcy, slave WIL 1
Mole, Lydia BAR 12
Molly, slave BAR 6
Molly, slave GEO 4
Molly, slave ORA 3
Molly, slave of Thos Bennett CHA 2
Molly, slave of E. H. Chamberlan EDG 1
Molly, slave of Julius Days EDG 5
Molly, slave of Robt Lamar EDG 14
Molly, slave of CHA 1 Dr. T. G. Prioleau
Molly, slave of Dr. A. N. Toomer CHA 6
Monday,slave COL 11
Monday, slave BAR 5
Monday, Ann F. EDG 4
Monk, slave UNI 3
Monroe, slave UNI 8
Montgomery, Hannah UNI 5
Montgomery, S. M. GRE 8
Moody, Charles C. SUM 8
Moody, Henrietta BAR 1
Moon, Virginia CHA 20
Mooney, M. R. NEW 2
Mooney, Pauline NEW 2
Moor, George, slave of LAU 6
Moore, infant AND 3
Moore,. Adolphus, slave KER 4
Moore, Caroline NEW 7
Moore, D. C., slave of ABB 16
Moore, J. T., slave of ABB 6
Moore, James NEW 7
Moore, James YRK 3
Moore, Jim, slave CFD 2
Moore, John, slave of AND 8
Moore, John M. EDG 7
Moore, M., slave of ABB 13
Moore, Martha T. EDG 9
Moore, Mary ABB 8
Moore, Reddin MRN 3
Moore, S. D. CHR 3
Moore, Sarah GRE 4
Moore, T., slave of ABB 17
Moore, William, slave YRK 5
Morehead, CarolineCHA 18
Moorehead, Henry AND 7
Morehead, Jane CHA 18
Moorer, Emily CHA 12
Moorer, Frances COL 5
Moorer, Mary CHA 12
Moorer, Rachel COL 5
Moragny, Isaac ABB 2
Morcock, Warwick, slave BEA 6
Morcock, Ralph, slave BEA 8
Mordic, slave GEO 1
Mordecai, Jasper CHA 24
Mordecai, Joe, slave CHA 21
Mordecai, Joseph CHA 24
More, slave SUM 12
Morehead, Henry B.PIC 6
Morgan, D., slave of UNI 1
Morgan, J. M. CHR 1
Morgan, Mary E. PIC 2
Morgan, Owen, slave of EDG 13
Morgan, Redin UNI 1
Morgan, Saleba FAI 3
Moriss, slave COL 7
Morn, James LAU 8
Morning, slave GRE 1
Morning, slave of Thomas McKie EDG 15
Morning, slave of Franklin Roper EDG 16
Morrah, Mary ABB 5
Morrah, S. R., slaves of ABB 3
Morris, slave YRK 3
Morris, slave BEA 12
Morris, slave COL 8
Morris, Daniel BAR 6
Morris, Dominick CHA 23
Morris, Elizabeth MRN 2
Morris, J. M. AND 7
Morris,Jefferson BAR 9
Morris, Joseph EDG 2
Morris, M. A., slaves of EDG 9
Morris, Sarah Ann BAR 2
Morrison, Catharine CFD 1
Morrison, John W. CHA 27
Morrison, W., slaves of ABB 15
Morrison, W., slave of ABB 9
Mortimer, John, slave CHA 25
Mose, slave YRK 1
Mose, slave of J. S. Adams ABB 16
Mose, slave of Jas McCelvey ABB 3
Mosely, Eliza BAR 4
Mosely, H., slave of ABB 18
Mosely, Nathaniel BAR 10
Mosely, T. P., slaves of ABB 16
Moses, slave BAR 10
Moses, slave BAR 11
Moses, slave SUM 13
Moses, slave SUM 1
Moses, slave WIL 1
Moses, slave GEO 1
Moses, slave UNI 5
Moses, slave UNI 4
Moses, slave of S. Acker AND 4
Moses, slave of Benj Coleman EDG 16
Moses, slave of J. McCarty EDG 18
Moses, slave of G. McDuffie ABB 13
Moses, slave of Wm. Mazyck CHA 11
Moses, slave of W. W. Walling EDG 2
Moses, Reuben CHA 21
Mosiah, slave of BEA 2 Dr. William C. Daniels
Mosley, Hugh, slaves of EDG 10
Mosly(?), Newman, slaves of EDG 13
Moss, Mary YRK 4
Moss, Mary J. FAI 2
Moss, Wm., slave of EDG 11
Motely, O., slave KER 1
Motes, Sarah, slave of LAU 6
Motts, Adam NEW 6
Mukins, Ann MBO 1
Mulligan, infant AND 4
Mullins, William CHA 15
Mullons, John CHA 16
Mungo, slave COL 2
Munro, Alexander CHA 26
Murdoch, Francis M ABB 8
Murdoch, Mary A. ABB 8
Murphey, Morris SUM 7
Murphey, Thomas GRE 8
Murray, slave MBO 2
Murray, Ann CHA 22
Murray, Ellen CHA 24
Murray, James CHA 24
Murray, Margaret A COL 1
Murree, Thos H., slaves of CHA 1
Murrell, William O CHA 19
Murry, Michael CHA 15
Muse, M. DAR 4
Myers, Catharine SUM 7
Myers, Sarah E., slave of FAI 5
Myers, Will, slave CHA 21
Myra, slave of Capt. Robertson CHA 2
Myrtilla, slave of T. W. Peyre CHA 3

Nace, slave BAR 3
Nacy, slave YRK 2
Nance, Elizabeth UNI 4
Nance, Elizabeth, slave of LAU 3
Nancy, William G NEW 4
Nancy, slave SUM 1
Nancy, slave BAR 3
Nancy, slave BAR 3
Nancy, slave BAR 1
Nancy, slave BAR 11
Nancy, slave CHA 10
Nancy, slave UNI 6
Nancy, slave LAN 1
Nancy, slave UNI 8

Nancy, slave NEW 2
Nancy, slave DAR 4
Nancy, slave DAR 3
Nancy, slave GEO 7
Nancy, slave WIL 1
Nancy, slave GEO 5
Nancy, slave COL 3
Nancy, slave COL 11
Nancy, slave COL 4
Nancy, slave COL 5
Nancy, slave COL 6
Nancy, slave WIL 4
Nancy, slave DAR 3
Nancy, slave YRK 4
Nancy, slave of AND 1
  James Armstrong
Nancy, slave of
  Wm Carter EDG 7
Nancy, slave of
  S. T. Gourdin CHA 13
Nancy, slave of
  J. H. Guerrard BEA 2
Nancy, slave of
  Wm Holmes EDG 11
Nancy, slave of
  John Jenings EDG 19
Nancy, slave of
  Edward Johnson UNI 2
Nancy, slave of
  A. W. Linch ABB 7
Nancy, slave of
  W. H. McCaw ABB 13
Nancy, slave of
  J. A. Martin ABB 8
Nancy, slave of
  S. S. Palmer CHA 9
Nancy,slave of
  F. W. Pickens EDG 8
Nancy, slave of
  C. S. Sims UNI 1
Nancy, slave of
  Amos Stallworth EDG 9
Nancy, slave of
  Dr. M. Waring CHA 2
Nanny, slave ORA 3
Nanny, slave BAR 14
Nanny, slave BAR 7
Nanny, slave BAR 4
Nanny, slave ORA 1
Nanny, slave GEO 3
Nanny, slave GEO 2
Nanney, slave GEO 6
Nanny, slave GEO 7
Nany, slave GEO 5
Naro, slave MRN 2
Nash, Sandy, slaveCHA 20
Nat, slave GEO 4
Nat, slave of
  D. Harris EDG 5
Nate, slave of
  J. W. Horst ABB 1
Nates, Andrew NEW 10
Nathan, slave NEW 3
Nathaniel, slave WIL 2
Neal, R. N. AND 3
Nebadnego, slave MBO 4
Ned, slave CHA 5
Ned, slave ORA 1
Ned, slave ORA 9
Ned, slave ORA 8
Ned, slave BEA 11
Ned, slave UNI 6
Ned, slave MBO 3
Ned, slave MRN 2
Ned, slave GEO 8
Ned, slave COL 10
Ned, slave COL 1
Ned, slave COL 9
Ned, slave of
  Wm. P. Ingraham CHA 1
Ned, slave of
  Stephen Jackson CFD 3
Ned, slave of
  E. Noble ABB 6
Ned, slave of
  Uriah Paulk UNI 2
Ned, slave of
  M. Ritchey ABB 12
Neel, Drucilla NEW 1
Neel, Rebecca NEW 1
Neighton, Ny.,
  slave KER 4
Neil, slave of FAI 1
Neil, James FAI 1
Neisinger, S.,
  slave KER 4
Nelly, slave ORA 2
Nelly, slave GEO 8
Nelly, slave YRK 1
Nelly, slave DAR 1
Nelly, slave CHA 12
Nelly, slave BAR 10
Nelly, slave MBO 4
Nelly, slave of CHA 6
  L. Haselden
Nelly, slave of
  James Reynolds EDG 17
Nelly, slave of
  Jonothan Tayler EDG 15
Nelson, slave BAR 8
Nelson, slave SUM 4
Nelson, slave BAR 4
Nelson, slave BAR 14
Nelson, slave MBO 1
Nelson, slave NEW 4
Nelson, slave MBO 3
Nelson, slave UNI 7
Nelson, slave MBO 1
Nelson, Elihu,
  slave LAU 6
Nelson, Icanah UNI 1
Nelson, Mary J. CHR 3
Nelson, William CHA 23
Nelson, Wm. R. AND 5
Nemo, slave BAR 8
Nen, slave of
  T. Weir ABB 11
Neptune, slave BAR 2
Nero, slave COL 9
Nero, slave COL 3
Nero, slave WIL 3
Nero, slave WIL 4
Nero, slave WIL 1
Nero, slave SUM 1
Nero, slave of
  F. A. Porcher CHA 2
Nesbit, A. LAN 2
Nesbit, H. G. W. LAN 2
Nesmith, Joseph T.WIL 4
Netts, William C. ABB 14
Netty, slave NEW 1
Nevil, Wm.,
  slave of AND 1
New, D., slaves of ABB 1
Newart, slave BAR 12
Newman, slave LAN 1
Newman, slave SUM 14
Newman, slave of
  A. Mazyck CHA 11
Newman, slave of
  John Miller EDG 2
Newman, Mary BAR 9
Newman, William GRE 2
Newton, slave SUM 7
Newton, slave of
  Kennon Breazeal AND 3
Newton, Elizabeth MBO 1
Newton, Sarah COL 7
Nichola, Adam CHA 23
Nicholson, Dr.,
  slave of EDG 8
Nicholson, S. W.,
  slave of EDG 6
Nick, slave UNI 7
Nickels, Elijah CHR 3
Nickels, ElizabethCHR 1
Nickols, James LAU 1
Nickols, John,
  slave of LAU 7
Nicy, slave LAN 2
Nicy, slave of
  B. Sale ABB 10
Nina, slave ORA 1
Nipper, Johnston,
  slaves of FAI 6
Nipper, TemperanceFAI 6
Nix, Berry PIC 4
Nix, Charles UNI 7
Noah, slave UNI 5
Noble, E.,
  slaves of ABB 6
Nobles, Zilpha EDG 6
Noe, James CHA 23
Norman, Robert UNI 7
Norman, Susan UNI 7
Normon, Samuel W. HOR 1
Norris, slave ORA 8
Norris, slave SUM 10
Norris, John JamesAND 5
Norris, John J. LAU 7
Norris, Mock BAR 3
Norris, Samuel EDG 9
Norris, Thomas HOR 1
North, Bess, slaveCHA 20
North, Thomas WIL 6
Northcut, T. DAR 4
Norwood, J. A.,
  slaves of ABB 5
Noveless, slave SPA 3
November, slave YRK 4
Nowel, slaves of CHA 10
Nunnery, Susan SUM 9

Oby, slave of
  Jos. R. Shelor PIC 6
OConnor, F.,
  slave of EDG 6
October, slave GEO 4
Odell, John,
  slaves of LAU 3
Odom, Larny BAR 9
Odom, Mary BAR 12
Odum, Wm GRE 4
Ogear, Sarah CHA 15
Ogelvy, Matthew CHA 24
OHara, Catharine CHA 21
Oland, John CHA 23
Old Bull, slave GEO 4
Old Tom, slave of CHA 3
  T. W. Porcher
Oldenburg, Caroline M.
  CHA 15
O Leary, Jery (?) YRK 2
Olive, slave ORA 3
Oliver, slave NEW 6
Oliver, David P. ORA 9
Oliver, James B. WIL 1
Oliver, John N. EDG 2
Olley, slave of
  M. Boulware FAI 1

Omarron, Mary CHA 20
O. Molly, slave of Jas. Ferguson CHA 1
Orange, slave BAR 1
Orr, J. L., slaves of AND 6
Oscar, slave NEW 7
Oscar, slave of E. Colliers Est. ABB 1
Oswald, John C. COL 2
Ouzts, Abram EDG 12
Ouzts, Daniel, family of EDG 5
Ouzts, Elizabeth, family of EDG 12
Ouzts, William EDG 12
Owen, slave BAR 12
Owen, Frederic AND 4
Owen, E., slaves of ABB 5
Owen, T. E., slave of ABB 5
Owens, Catharine MRN 1
Owens, Clara CHA 27
Owens, Edward CHA 27
Owens, James BAR 8
Owens, John LAU 8
Owens, Lucy BAR 7
Owens, Mary M. WIL 3
Owens, Sam H., slaves of FAI 7
Owen, Sarah AND 4
Owens, Sarah PIC 4
Owens, Susannah WIL 3
Owens, Tracy MRN 2
Owensby, Jas., slave of EDG 13
Oxendine, Fielding SUM 9
Oxner, infant FAI 4
Oxner, George H. NEW 5
Oxner, Wesley B. NEW 5
Oxxy, slave MRN 2

Pace, Sarah, slaves of ABB 12
Pack, David SUM 5
Pack, George AND 1
Packman, Charles, slaves of EDG 1
Paden, Alex GRE 6
Paden, Nancy GRE 3
Paden, Robt GRE 6
Paden, T. T. GRE 6
Padget, T. E., family of EDG 6
Page, Thomas UNI 1
Page, Thomas UNI 5
Page, Wm., slave LAU 5
Pagett, Marcelus E. EDG 18
Pale, Martin SUM 12
Pally, slave of T. W. Porcher CHA 3
Palmer, Dr., slaves of CHA 3
Palmer, Dr. J. S., slave of CHA 13
Palmer, M. H. CHA 13
Palmer, Martha UNI 1
Palmer, R. N., slave of ABB 5
Palmer, S. W., slaves of CHA 13
Palmer, S. C., slaves of CHA 9
Palmer, William ABB 1
Palty, slave of P. F. Cleckley ABB 8
Pamelia, slave of W. Williams EDG 7
Panigh(?), Arthur, slave YRK 5
Pansin, Eliza, slave CHA 26
Paris, P. CHA 10
Parish, Nancy MBO 1
Park, Sarah L. CHR 5
Parker, Daniel, slave YRK 5
Parker, Daniel J. HOR 1
Parker, Ellen L., slave of ABB 5
Parker, Harriet, slave CHA 19
Parker, Henry CHA 16
Parker, Nancy MBO 2
Parker, Rud, slave KER 1
Parker, Sarah Jane CFD 2
Parker, William MBO 2
Parkman, John EDG 12
Parks, Davis J. YRK 4
Parks, James, slaves of LAU 9
Parmlee, Ann GRE 8
Paro, slave of A. Mazyck CHA 11
Parr, Mary UNI 1
Parrot, slave GEO 3
Parthenia, slave UNI 6
Parthenia, slave of S. B. Brooks ABB 11
Partlow, J. S., slave of ABB 11
Partlow, J. Y., slave of ABB 19
Pat, slave of Robt Jennings EDG 13
Paterson, James PIC 5
Patience, slave SUM 10
Patience, slave of W. J. Hanna CFD 1
Patience, slave of Stephen Wilson EDG 14
Patric, slave of William Kelly UNI 2
Patsey, slave of John Jennings UNI 1
Patrick, slave of J. Watson ABB 10
Patrick, C. R., slave COL 3
Patsey, slave WIL 3
Patsey, slave GEO 5
Patsy, slave UNI 4
Patsey, slave NEW 6
Patsey, slave of John Jennings UNI 1
Patsey, slave of Robt Jennings EDG 13
Patsey, slave of Waddy Thompson EDG 8
Patty, slave of William Thurmond EDG 1
Patterson, Emiline, slave KER 1
Patterson, George, slave BEA 6
Patterson, George, slave KER 1
Patterson, Harriet, slave KER 1
Patterson, Ima, slave KER 1
Patterson, James ABB 1
Patterson, L. J., slave of ABB 2
Patterson, Letty, slave KER 1
Patterson, Patty, slave KER 1
Patterson, Peter, slave KER 1
Patterson, Susan YRK 3
Patterson, Wm., slave BEA 6
Patton, Elizabeth PIC 2
Patton, Henry KER 4
Patton, Thomas B. YRK 4
Patty, slave CHA 10
Patty, slave COL 11
Patty, slave COL 11
Patty, slave of J. C. Ball CHA 2
Patty, slave of John F. Middleton EDG 15
Patty, slave of Dr. T. G. Prioleau CHA 1
Paul, slave GRE 2
Paul, slave COL 10
Paul, slave BAR 1
Paul, slave CHA 5
Paul, slave of Wm. Ducass CHA 9
Paul, slave of T. C. Haskill ABB 17
Paul, slave of Wm. Mazyck CHA 11
Paul, slave of Dr. J. S. Palmer CHA 13
Paul, slave of S. S. Palmer CHA 9
Paulina, slave NEW 7
Pauline, slave of S. Bowker UNI 2
Paulk, Uriah, slave of UNI 2
Pauls, slave GEO 5
Payton, slave NEW 4
Peagler, D., slave of CHA 13
Pearson, George B., slave of FAI 4
Peay, John E., slaves of FAI 5
Peay, Nicholas A., slaves of FAI 5
Peeples, Wyley, slave of BEA 14
Peg, slave COL 9
Peg, slave of E. Laroche CHA 6
Peggy, slave CHA 14
Peggy, slave SUM 12
Peggy, slave CHA 12
Peggy, slave CHA 10
Peggy, slave WIL 2
Peggy, slave SUM 6
Peggy, slave DAR 3
Peggy, slave GEO 1
Peggy, slave GEO 2
Peggy, slave GEO 8
Peggy, slave ORA 4
Peggy, slave ORA 3
Peggy, slave of Martha Hughes ABB 6
Peggy, slave of W. Long Jr. ABB 14
Pelgrum, J. F. SPA 3

Pendah, slave GEO 1
Pendarvis, Lewis COL 5
Penny, slave BAR 3
Penny, slave of Robt D. Killin CFD 1
Penny, slave of G. McDuffie ABB 13
Penny, slave of Jane Smith FAI 1
Penny, Elizabeth F. ABB 7
Penwell, Eliza BAR 5
Perdue, William CFD 1
Perkins, Catharine EDG 8
Perkins, Elizabeth ABB 12
Perkins, Elizabeth EDG 8
Perkins, Milton EDG 8
Permela, slave GRE 4
Permelia, slave NEW 9
Permelia, slave NEW 3
Perrin, J. P. EDG 6
Perry, slave of Peter Johnson AND 2
Perry, slave of W. Ritchey ABB 14
Perry, E. W., slave of EDG 3
Perry, Mary, slave of EDG 3
Perry, John, slaves of KER 1
Perry, Susan YRK 1
Perry, Wm., slave KER 2
Perryclear, Jack, slave BEA 8
Pervis, John, slave of CFD 2
Peter, slave LAN 2
Peter, slave GRE 8
Peter, slave SUM 8
Peter, slave SUM 7
Peter, slave SUM 4
Peter, slave SUM 3
Peter, slave SUM 2
Peter, slave GRE 1
Peter, slave WIL 5
Peter, slave WIL 4
Peter, slave COL 10
Peter, slave COL 12
Peter, slave COL 7
Peter, slave COL 2
Peter, slave GEO 1
Peter, slave WIL 4
Peter, slave CHA 14
Peter, slave BAR 12
Peter, slave BAR 9
Peter, slave GEO 1
Peter, slave GEO 4
Peter, slave MBO 1
Peter, slave MRN 3
Peter, slave ORA 1
Peter, slave ORA 7
Peter, slave of J. C. Ball CHA 2
Peter, slave of J. Cothran ABB 1
Peter, slave of Lewis Crouch EDG 19
Peter, slave of John Doby EDG 16
Peter, slave of T. R. Garey ABB 16
Peter, slave of T. C. Griffin ABB 15
Peter, slave of J. Hightower EDG 14
Peter, slave of Thos Hill EDG 18
Peter, slave of WM. Martin AND 3
Peter, slave of G. McDuffie ABB 13
Peter, slave of J. B. Richey ABB 15
Peter Joe, slave of F. W. PickensEDG 8
Peters, Amelia (free mulatto) CHA 27
Peters, Barbara COL 5
Peters, Edward CHA 15
Peters, Sinkley COL 5
Peterson, C., slave of EDG 7
Peterson, Louisa CHA 27
Petigru, T., slave of ABB 17
Petska, David CHA 22
Pettigrew, John W.FAI 4
Pettigru, James, slave CHA 24
Pettypool--see Pool
Peurefoy, Margaret
Peyre, T. W., L. CHA 26
slave of CHA 4
Peyre, T. W., slave of CHA 3
Phactow, slave GEO 5
Phebe, slave GRE 1
Phebe, slave GEO 3
Phebe, slave GEO 7
Phebe, slave MBO 2
Phebe, slave MBO 3
Pheby, slave SUM 7
Pheby, slave SUM 13
Phebe,slave MBO 4
Phebe, slave NEW 2
Phebe, slave of Moses Holstun EDG 19
Pheby, slave SUM 11
Philip, slave COL 12
Philip , slave BEA 12
Philip , slave HOR 2
Phillips, slave LAN 2
Philips, Eliza J. UNI 8
Phillips, M. R. LAN 1
Philips, Narcissa AND 7
Phillips, R. LAN 1
Philips, Sarah L. LAU 9
Philips, William AND 7
Philis, slave ORA 2
Philis, slave SPA 4
Phill, slave SUM 1
Phillip, slave of John Rainsford EDG 16
Phillip, slave YRK 2
Phillips, Elijah PIC 6
Phillips, John L. LAU 7
Phillips, Marion CHA 26
Phillips, Martha CHA 26
Phillis, slave SUM 3
Phillis, slave SUM 2
Phillis, slave GEO 8
Phillis, slave MRN 1
Phillis, slave GEO 4
Phillis, slave GEO 2
Phillis, slave GEO 1
Phillis, slave WIL 5
Phillis, slave ORA 3
Phillis, slave ORA 3
Phillis, slave BAR 8
Phillis, slave BAR 14
Phillis, slave LAN 3
Phillis, slave LAN 2
Phillis, slave of A. A. Hunter ABB 12
Phillis, slave of Thos Jones EDG 5
Phillis, slave of W. Morrison ABB 15
Phillis, slave of Mary Perry EDG 3
Philm, Elizh. KER 3
Philson, James W. LAU 2
Phinny, Sinclair LAU 1
Phoeba, slave of Jane Turner EDG 9
Phoeba, slave of B. Jordan ABB 9
Phoebe, slave of John YoungbloodEDG 7
Phyllis, slave of T. W. Porcher CHA 3
Phyllis, slave of Dr. M. Waring CHA 2
Pickell, Caroline AND 4
Pickens, F. W., slaves of EDG 8
Pickett, John FAI 1
Pickett, Kelley WIL 2
Pickett, Nancy FAI 1
Pinckney, slave SPA 3
Pinckney, C. C., slave of CHA 10
Pinckney, Henry Frost CHA 24
Pinckney, Col. Thos. Est. of CHA 10
Pinkey, slave of Saml Clarke EDG 2
Pittman, Francis ABB 5
Pitts, Ephraim, slaves of LAU 4
Pivan, slave BAR 13
Plair, Miss CHA 13
Plane, slave of Dr. William Daniels BEA 2
Pleasant, slave NEW 10
Plumly, Franklin GRE 8
Plute, slave MBO 2
Poag, Joseph CHR 4
Polatta, WhitfieldEDG 7
Polly, slave SUM 5
Polly, slave HOR 1
Polly, slave GEO 6
Polly, slave GEO 4
Polly, slave DAR 4
Polly, slave DAR 3
Polly, slave BAR 8
Polly, slave DAR 2
Polly, slave of G. W. Duvall CFD 2
Polly, slave of Dr. Palmer CHA 3
Polly, slave of L. Reynolds ABB 10
Polly, slave of J. Wideman ABB 4
Polydon, slave of Dr. S. W. Barker CHA 1
Polydore, slave CHA 13
Pompey, slave MBO 2
Pompey, slave GEO 8
Pompey, slave of Yarborough Broadwater EDG 16
Pompey, slave of K. Simmes Sr. CHA 1
Pompy, slave COL 9
Pool, A. P., slave ABB 18

Pool, Edward SUM 14
Pool, Peter P. LAU 4
Pope, Abey, slave BEA 8
Pope, Allick, slave BEA 7
Pope, Carrie H. BEA 12
Pope, Jacob EDG 19
Pope, Peter, slave BEA 8
Pope, Rachel, slave BEA 7
Poplin, Martha CFD 3
Poppenheim, slave of CHA 12
Poppenheim, Berry, slave CHA 25
Porcher, F. A., slaves of CHA 2
Porcher, Mr. Isaac CHA 4
Porcher, Saml, slaves of CHA 13
Porcher, T. W., slaves of CHA 3
Porcher, Thos Est., slaves of CHA 3
Porcher, Wm. E., slaves of CHA 2
Pork, Jonas LAU 4
Porter, J. LAN 3
Porter, James BAR 1
Porter, Margaret SPA 1
Porter, Martha M. ORA 2
Porter, S. Ann SPA 1
Porterfield, Polly A. ABB 5
Porterfield, Willis ABB 5
Porteous, John, slave BEA 7
Porteous, Mary, slave BEA 7
Posey, Agnes ABB 6
Posey, Martin (executed) EDG 11
Poston, John MRN 1
Posy(?), Newman LAU 7
Potter, J. O. HOR 2
Potter, Mary HOR 2
Poulson, Emanuel CFD 2
Pow, Jacob EDG 11
Powe, Martha, slave of CFD 2
Powe, T. E., slave of CFD 2
Powell, Sanford LAU 4
Power, Drury PIC 2
Power, Elizabeth GRE 4
Poyas, Toby, slave CHA 15
Prat, J., slave of ABB 15
Prater, Hesekiah LEX 3
Pratt, E., slave of ABB 14
Prenius(?), Mimmy (mulatto) COL 5
Prescott, Daniel, slave of EDG 1
Prescott, William, slaves of EDG 16
Presley, Mary B. WIL 4
Pressley, G. W., slave of ABB 2
Preston, slave NEW 7
Preston, slave of D. Harris EDG 5
Prewit, Frances S. AND 1

Price, Charles J. EDG 8
Price, Eliza Ann AND 5
Price, Sydney BAR 10
Priestor, Benjamin BAR 3
Priestor, Josiah BAR 3
Priestor, Sophora BAR 11
Primus, slave BAR 10
Primus, slave GEO 8
Primus, slave of J. Harleston CHA 7
Primus, slave of R. N. Palmer ABB 5
Primus, slave of Henry L. Stevens CHA 2
Prince, slave UNI 7
Prince, slave BEA 13
Prince, slave GRE 2
Prince, slave WIL 3
Prince, slave SUM 3
Prince, slave SUM 6
Prince, slave COL 9
Prince, slave NEW 7
Prince, slave of J. B. Bull ABB 2
Prince, slave of Thomas G. Lamar EDG 14
Prince, H. M., slaves of ABB 7
Prince, Mary HOR 2
Pringle, J. J., slaves of BEA 3
Pringle, John SUM 1
Prioleau, Dr., T. F., slaves of CHA 1
Prior, Charlott, slave of EDG 2
Prior, Joseph, slave LAU 5
Priscilla, slave SUM 4
Priscilla, slave of John M. Clark EDG 1
Pritchard, Columbia CHA 18
Pritchard, Henry W. CHA 18
Pritchard, John H. CHA 18
Pritchett, Martha GRE 3
Proby, slave GEO 4
Proctor, scriven BEA 11
Prot, John Jr. ABB 14
Prother, J. W., slaves of ABB 3
Provost, John (mulatto) COL 2
Puckett, Cornelius, slave of LAU 2
Pulaski, slave of Benjn Coleman EDG 16
Purdy, James ABB 7
Purifoy, Tilmon D., slave of EDG 19
Purse, William A. CHA 26
Putnam, Abner F. LAU 7
Purvis, Edward CHA 18
Pyatt, Robert, slave CHA 25
Pyatt, Susan, slave CHA 25
Pyland, Edward EDG 20

Quaces, slave COL 11
Quail, Catherine CHA 26
Quail, Francis CHA 26
Quail, John CHA 22
Quash, Albert CHA 18
Quattlebum, Thomas, slave LEX 3
Queen Ann, slave of W. B. Brooks ABB 11
Quick, Mary MBO 1
Quillen, John B. BAR 10
Quilter, John CHA 19
Quitman, slave BAR 8
Quitman, Ann CHA 23
Quomba, slave CHA 10

Rabe, Charles A. GRE 8
Rabun, Willis HOR 2
Rachael, slave BEA 11
Rachael, slave of James Gaillard Sr. CHA 3
Rachael, slave of Miss Hamlin CHA 6
Rachael, slave of Capt. Nathan Johnson BEA 1
Rachal, slave NEW 2
Rachel, slave SUM 13
Rachel, slave WIL 1
Rachel, slave HOR 1
Rachel, slave GEO 8
Rachel, slave GEO 6
Rachel, slave COL 7
Rachel, slave SUM 5
Rachel, slave YRK 4
Rachel, slave SUM 3
Rachel, slave SUM 2
Rachel, slave GRE 5
Rachel, slave GRE 8
Rachel, slave BAR 4
Rachel, slave NEW 1
Rachel, slave ORA 2
Rachel, slave of Julius Days EDG 5
Rachel, slave of D. Lesly ABB 6
Rachel, slave of A. Logan ABB 11
Rachel, slave of J. Watsons Est. ABB 10
Rachel, slave of W. L. Wharton ABB 9
Rackley, Elzara PIC 2
Raiborn, Emaline EDG 5
Raiborn, H., family of EDG 5
Rainsford, John, slave of EDG 16
Rall, Barbara, slave LEX 2
Ralph, slave NEW 3
Ralph, slave of J. Dorn EDG 7
Ralph, slave of F. W. Pickens EDG 9
Rambo, A. J., slave of EDG 2
Rampey, Martha EDG 10
Rampy, Syntha C. PIC 2
Ramsden, Mary E. CHA 24
Ramsey, John CHA 24
Ramsey, William COL 2
Ramy, slave of J. Aiken ABB 7
Ramy, slave of Tandy Burkhalter EDG 1
Randal, slave FAI 2
Randal, slave of G. McDuffie ABB 13
Randal, slave of S. W. Nicholson EDG 6

Randal, slave of T. E. Owen ABB 5
Randall, Robt BAR 10
Randle, Ann CHA 19
Randle, John CHA 23
Randol, slave of B. Talbert ABB 1
Ranse, Peter CHA 17
Ranse, Robert CHA 17
Ransier, Joseph CHA 23
Ransom, slave BAR 3
Ransom, slave SUM 13
Ransy, slave of Jacob Mangum CFD 3
Ratcliff, slave GEO 8
Ratteree, N. F. CHR 1
Rauch, Jacob LEX 1
Raukel(?), William LEX 1
Ravenel, Catharine CHA 15
Ravenel, Henry W., slave of CHA 1
Ravenel, Miss Maria CHA 4
Ravenel, Thomas P., slave of CHA 2
Ray, infant slave RIC 1
Ray, Ambrose UNI 8
Ray, James R., slave of LAU 6
Ray, Jane BAR 3
Ray, Louisa ABB 5
Ray, Mary UNI 8
Ray, Sarah BAR 11
Rayborn, Elizabeth ABB 9
Rayborn, Jane M. ABB 11
Raymond, slave SUM 13
Raysor, J. C., slave of ABB 12
Ready(?), Henry BAR 14
Ready, Mary BAR 14
Reagin, Catharine ABB 1
Reagin, Jesse ABB 1
Reagin, Rachel ABB 1
Rearden, Joseph, slaves of EDG 12
Reaves, Emiline PIC 4
Rebecca, slave GEO 8
Rebecca, slave BAR 2
Rebecca, slave GEO 8
Rebecca, slave COL 3
Rebecca, slave COL 9
Rebecca, slave COL 10
Rebecca, slave NEW 2
Rebecca, slave YRK 2
Rebecca, slave GRE 3
Rebecca, slave FAI 6
Rebecca, slave NEW 1
Rebecca, slave of J. E. Allen AND 1
Rebecca, slave of CHA 13 W. D. Villeponteaux
Rector, Elizabeth GRE 1
Red, infant BAR 9
Red, James H. ABB 9
Redd, Daniel NEW 9
Redd, Elizabeth NEW 5
Redd, William NEW 5
Reece, H., slave of AND 1
Reed, Ann BAR 6
Reed, John W. ABB 4
Reeder, Sarah A. M. CHA 25
Reese, slave COL 3
Reese, slave WIL 1
Reese, Giles, slave RIC 1
Reese, Judith, slave RIC 1
Reese, Margaret, slave RIC 1
Reese, Rosa, slave RIC 1
Reese, Wm. J. SUM 8
Reeves, James COL 5
Reeves, Joseph COL 5
Reeves, Letitia PIC 2
Regina, slave of J. F. Feaster FAI 8
Reid, A., slave of AND 5
Reid, F. M. PIC 4
Reid, J. S., slaves of ABB 5
Reid, L., slave of ABB 7
Reid, Mary E. PIC 4
Reid, S., slave of ABB 15
Reid, Saml, slave of PIC 5
Reitt, slave CHA 10
Remob, slave CHA 10
Renty, slave GEO 1
Renty, slave BAR 14
Renty, slave BAR 8
Renty, slave BEA 11
Renty, slave BAR 11
Rentz, Emanuel BAR 11
Renwick, Melissa J. NEW 7
Renwick, Rosanna T. UNI 7
Reuben, slave FAI 6
Reuben, slave MBO 2
Reuben, slave of Wm. A. Carson CHA 1
Reuben, slave of B. Haygood FAI 8
Reuben, slave of William Prescott EDG 16
Revills, E. DAR 3
Reynolds, Eugene EDG 12
Reynolds, George EDG 12
Reynolds, James, slave of EDG 17
Reynolds, John, slave of EDG 17
Reynolds, Joseph, slave BEA 6
Reynolds, L., slaves of ABB 10
Reynolds, Lewis, family of EDG 12
Reynolds, Rachel, slave BEA 6
Rhame, Mary T. SUM 9
Rhemas, slave COL 10
Rhett, Hector, slave BEA 7
Rhoda, slave NEW 4
Rhoda, slave of O. Kennedy FAI 1
Rhoden, George EDG 20
Rhoden, Kennerly EDG 18
Rhodes, L. J., slaves of LAU 6
Rias, slave ORA 1
Rice, Ben BAR 13
Rice, F., slave of AND 8
Rice, Ibzan, slave of AND 6
Rice, Mary BAR 4
Rich, slave of Al. Douglas FAI 3
Richard (free black) WIL 3
Richard, slave BAR 9
Richard, slave CHA 12
Richard, slave COL 5
Richard, slave BEA 11
Richard, slave GRE 3
Richard, slave of Wm. P. Ingraham CHA 1
Richard, slave of W. H. McCar ABB 13
Richard, slave SUM 7
Richard, slave SUM 9
Richard, slave SUM 10
Richd, slave SUM 13
Richards, James SPA 1
Richards, Thomas CHA 24
Richardson, Jefferson EDG 10
Richardson, L. KER 4
Richardson, Mary, slave BEA 8
Richardson, Richard SUM 5
Richardson, Sallie, slave of EDG 10
Richardson, Susan, slave BEA 8
Richardson, Wm. G. SUM 8
Richburgh, Erom(?) SUM 3
Richey, A., slave of ABB 7
Richey, J. B., slaves of ABB 15
Richey, M. V., slave of ABB 16
Richey, Martha ABB 15
Richey, Robert ABB 15
Richmond, slave NEW 1
Ridgell, Luther M. SUM 4
Ridgeway, Jas. SUM 1
Ridgeway, Joseph S. SUM 2
Ridgeway, Saml E. SUM 2
Ridlehuber, John NEW 7
Ridlehuber, Simmion LEX 3
Rigby, Dr. John ORA 6
Riggs, Edward, slave CHA 15
Riggs, Henry, slave CHA 19
Riggs, Susan, slave CHA 15
Riggs, Susan, slave CHA 19
Rigsby, Richd COL 5
Riley, Eliza BAR 14
Riley, J., slave of ABB 9
Riley, James LAU 7
Riley, Rachel BAR 1
Rilly, slave of Thos Bennett CHA 2
Rina, slave GEO 1
Rina, slave BAR 8
Rinah, slave COL 3
Ripley, Jane, slave CHA 20
Riser, S. L. NEW 7
Ritchey, Elizabeth J. ABB 17
Ritchey, Elizabeth N. ABB 15
Ritchey, J. W., slave of ABB 14
Ritchey, M., slaves of ABB 12

Ritchey, Parthenia ABB 14
Ritchey, Robert C. ABB 15
Ritchie, R. C., slave of ABB 15
Ritta, slave UNI 7
Ritter, slave of Archy Clarke EDG 4
Ritty, slave MBO 1
River(?), Susannah EDG 4
Rivers, George BEA 14
Rivers, Penelope SUM 5
Rivers, Reuben BAR 7
Rivers, Susan CHA 15
Robbins, Rachel, slave CHA 22
Roberson, James CHA 16
Roberson, Lewis, slave LEX 3
Robert, slave WIL 3
Robert, slave BAR 10
Robert, slave CHA 5
Robert, slave WIL 3
Robert, slave GEO 8
Robert, slave GEO 7
Robert, slave GEO 5
Robert, slave WIL 2
Robert, slave COL 11
Robert, slave NEW 1
Robert, slave NEW 3
Robert, slave NEW 9
Robert, slave FAI 2
Robert, slave FAI 1
Robert, slave UNI 3
Robert, slave LAN 1
Robert C---, slave YRK 5
Robert, slave of M. B. Clark ABB 13
Robert, slave of J. McCord ABB 9
Robert, slave of O. Towles EDG 7
Robt, slave of Saml Porcher CHA 13
Roberts, Absolam ABB 3
Roberts, Benj. BAR 8
Roberts, E., family of EDG 12
Roberts, Eliz. BAR 14
Roberts, J. M. GRE 8
Roberts, M., slaves of AND 2
Roberts, Samuel GRE 2
Roberts, Shelton G. EDG 12
Robertson, slave ORA 3
Robertson, Abram EDG 17
Roberts, Capt., slaves of CHA 2
Robertson, Douglas, slave of EDG 3
Robertson, Elisha EDG 10
Robertson, Elisha, slave of EDG 10
Robertson, Elizabeth EDG 13
Robertson, Eve EDG 14
Robertson, J. C., slave of EDG 13
Robertson, John AND 2
Robertson, John, slave of FAI 2
Robertson, Lewis EDG 10
Robertson, Martha F. FAI 4
Robertson, MicajahEDG 10
Robertson, Nancy EDG 10
Robertson, T. A. LAN 4
Robertson, W. C., slave of EDG 4
Robeson,Thos W., slaves of CFD 1
Robin, slave UNI 3
Robin, slave ORA 9
Robin, slave BAR 3
Robinson, A. LAN 3
Robinson, Annie ABB 3
Robinson, Benj M. ABB 14
Robinson, Elisha PIC 4
Robinson, George W. PIC 4
Robinson, IsabellaABB 1
Robinson, J., slave of ABB 1
Robinson, J. P., slave of FAI 1
Robinson, James BEA 11
Robinson, Jane, slave CHA 25
Robinson, John A. AND 5
Robinson, John J. FAI 1
Robinson, Joseph, slave CHA 25
Robinson, Madison BAR 2
Robinson, R., slaves of ABB 17
Robinson, Richard, slave CHA 25
Robinson, S. Ann GEO 2
Robinson, William ABB 3
Robinson, Yongue FAI 8
Roche, Thomas ABB 5
Rochell, John W., slave of EDG 17
Roda, slave COL 9
Roda, slave GEO 3
Roddy, Martin JunrCHA 18
Roddy, Martin SenrCHA 18
Rogers, D. M., slave of ABB 4
Rodgers, John LAU 8
Rodgers, Margaret WIL 2
Rogers, P., slave of ABB 3
Rodgers, William AND 3
Rody, Briget CHA 18
Rogers, Mary CHA 18
Rogers, Saml CHA 24
Rogers, William PIC 6
Roland, Isabella ABB 17
Roland, Mary J. ABB 17
Rollings, W. W., slave of FAI 5
Rolly, slave of John Glover FAI 3
Romedy, Joseph FAI 6
Romeo, slave CHA 5
Ronty, slave BAR 9
Rook, James L. NEW 7
Rook, Thos J., slave of LAU 2
Roper, Eliza CHA 19
Roper, Franklin, slave of EDG 16
Roper, Jane PIC 3
Roper, Susan A., Slave of EDG 16
Rosa, slave SPA 3
Rosanna, slave of D. R. Coleman FAI 3
Rosanna, slave of G. Sibert ABB 1
Rose, slave YRK 3
Rose, slave ORA 9
Rose, slave BAR 11
Rose, slave BAR 12
Rose, slave BAR 13
Rose, slave SUM 10
Rose, slave SUM 11
Rose, slave SUM 8
Rose, slave SUM 7
Rose, slave SUM 1
Rose, slave COL 10
Rose, slave COL 9
Rose, slave GEO 2
Rose, slave GEO 6
Rose, slave RIC 2
Rose, slave MRN 1
Rose, slave MBO 1
Rose, slave WIL 1
Rose, slave SUM 11
Rose, slave UNI 4
Rose, slave LAN 4
Rose, slave LAN 2
Rose, slave LAN 1
Rose, slave of E. R. Calhoun ABB 11
Rose, slave of R. N. Graves ABB 13
Rose, slave of A. Harris ABB 18
Rose, slave of Joseph Jennings EDG 4
Rose, slave of J. McCord ABB 9
Rose, slave of M. S. Mann ABB 6
Rose, slave of F. Oconnor EDG 6
Rose, slave of John Reynolds EDG 17
Rose, slave of F. H. Wardlaw EDG 11
Roseborough, R. R., slave of FAI 8
Rose, Hugh, slave of BEA 2
Rose, Margaret CHA 21
Rose, Maria, slave BEA 9
Rose, Matilda, slave BEA 9
Rosette, slave of T. Thompson ABB 5
Ross, slave RIC 2
Ross, Adam, slave CHA 22
Ross, C. H. LAN 2
Ross, William, slave of AND 4
Ross, Willis BAR 8
Rothrock, Frances E. ABB 16
Rountree, Asa BAR 7
Rountree, William J., slave of EDG 14
Rowe, Mary M. EDG 19
Rowell, H. LAN 3
Root, Jas. KER 4
Rowell, Jonas COL 2
Rowell, Rily BAR 11
Rowland, Wm GRE 5
Roxana, slave of Gilbert Tenant EDG 15
Rucker, James H., slave LEX 4
Rudamer, J. ORA 4
Rudd, D., slave of ABB 19
Rudd, Lucinda NEW 3

Rudy, John CHA 15
Ruff, Ann Eliza NEW 2
Ruff, C. Est., slaves of ABB 15
Ruff, Claiborne NEW 2
Rufus, slave NEW 10
Rummy, slave CHA 10
Rumph, Senator COL 5
Rumph, Wm. COL 8
Runnells, A. GRE 1
Runnells, J. DAR 3
Runnels, Mary BAR 4
Rush, Caroline CHA 17
Rush, L. ORA 3
Rubin, slave of D. D. Brunson EDG 17
Rucker, Henry, slave of EDG 19
Rumbey, Joseph EDG 14
Russel, slave GEO 7
Ruth, Nathaniel G., slave of BEA 1
Rutherford, Joseph E., slave of EDG 19
Rutherford, Mary Ann CHA 24
Rutherford, Thomas CHA 24
Rutledge, Mrs., slaves of CHA 11
Rutledge, John, slave of BEA 2
Rutlege, David, slave CHA 19
Ryan, John CHA 23

Sabb, Eliza W. SUM 3
Sabe, slave of Mark. B. Whittle EDG 19
Sabra, slave MBO 4
Sabrina, slave BAR 5
Saby, slave of A. McClellan CHA 9
Sachtlebeu, Henry M. CHA 27
Sachtlebeu, Sarah M. CHA 27
Sackladen, Mary CHA 22
Sader, Eugena M. A. CHA 21
Sadler, Neng GoldYRK 2
Sagilla, slave MBO 4
Sale, B., slaves of ABB 10
Sall, slave SPA 1
Sall, J., slave of ABB 17
Sall, J., slave of ABB 18
Sally, slave BAR 10
Sally, slave COL 3
Sally, slave COL 4
Sally, slave COL 8
Sally, slave COL 10
Sally, slave COL 11
Sally, slave DAR 1
Sally, slave DAR 2
Sally, slave DAR 3
Sally, slave FAI 7
Sally, slave GEO 4
Sally, slave GRE 1
Sally, slave MBO 1
Sally, slave MRN 1
Sally, slave MRN 3
Sally, slave ORA 2
Sally, slave ORA 4
Sally, slave ORA 8
Sally, slave SUM 9
Sally, slave SUM 13
Sally, slave UNI 7
Sally, slave WIL 4
Sally, slave WIL 5
Sally, slave of W. P. Brooks ABB 10
Sally, slave of T. Chatham ABB 11
Sally, slave of Langdon Chevis BEA 2
Sally, slave of V. Griffins Est. ABB 10
Sally, slave of M. Jerman CHA 9
Sally, slave of C. Manigault CHA 7
Sally, slave of Charles Packman EDG 1
Sally, slave of G. W. Pressley ABB 2
Sally, slave of Alex Sharpton EDG 15
Sally, Thos, family of EDG 11
Sam, slave BAR 1
Sam, slave BAR 3
Sam, slave BAR 8
Sam, slave BAR 9
Sam, slave COL 4
Sam, slave COL 5
Sam, slave COL 7
Sam, slave COL 8
Sam, slave COL 11
Sam, slave DAR 1
Sam, slave DAR 2
Sam, slave DAR 2
Sam, slave FAI 4
Sam, slave GEO 2
Sam, slave GEO 3
Sam, slave GEO 4
Sam, slave GEO 8
Sam, slave HOR 3
Sam, slave MRN 3
Sam, slave ORA 8
Sam, slave WIL 1
Sam, slave YRK 1
Sam, slave YRK 2
Sam, slave YRK 3
Sam, slave of Elizabeth Burress EDG 1
Sam, slave of J. M. Carson ABB 9
Sam, slave of Reubin Cooper EDG 8
Sam, slave of Benjamin DouthitAND 3
Sam, slave of W. T. Drennan ABB 3
Sam, slave of W. Morrison ABB 15
Sam, slave of J. S. Reid ABB 5
Sam, slave of J.Robinson ABB 1
Sam, slave of Nathaniel G. Ruth BEA 1
Sam, slave of Dr. J. P. Scriven BEA 2
Sam, slave of M. C. Tallman ABB 4
Sambo, slave BAR 1
Sambo, slave BAR 13
Sambo, slave MBO 2
Samo, slave UNI 8
Samk, slave BAR 3
Sampson, slave CHA 10
Sampson, slave MRN 1
Sampson, slave SUM 8
Sampson, slave SUM 1
Sampson, slave FAI 2
Sampson, slave FAI 7
Sampson, slave of R. Brady ABB 3
Sampson, slave of Elisha StevenEDG 7
Sampson,slave of W. J. Taylor ABB 4
Sams, Affy, slave BEA 7
Sams, Albert, slave BEA 7
Sams, Alpha, slave BEA 6
Sams, Bainbridge BEA 10
Sams, Billy, slave BEA 6
Sams, Mary, slave BEA 7
Sams, Minta, slave BEA 6
Sams, Pompey, slave BEA 7
Sams, Rachel, slave BEA 6
Sams, Rachel, slave BEA 7
Sams, Renty, slave BEA 7
Sams, Robert, slave BEA 6
Sams, Robin, slave BEA 7
Samuel, slave LAN 3
Samuel, slave NEW 1
Samuel, slave NEW 3
Samuel, slave NEW 6
Samuel, slave NEW 8
Samuel, slave NEW 10
Samuel, slave SUM 4
Samuel, slave SUM 10
Saml, slave DAR 3
Saml, slave SPA 1
Samuel, Elizabeth, slave of EDG 16
Samuel, Mewco, slave of EDG 16
Samuel, slave of Henry W. Ravenel CHA 1
Samuel, slave of D. Steen UNI 2
Samy, slave of Ellington Searle EDG 13
Sancho, slave BAR 7
Sandefer, William A. YRK 3
Sanders, Johnson BAR 9
Sanders, Levi CHR 1
Sanders, Rutha EDG 3
Sanders, Taylor COL 2
Sanders, Martha KER 4
Sandy, slave BAR 7
Sandy, slave BAR 7
Sandy, slave DAR 1
Sandy, slave NEW 4
Sandy, slave WIL 2
Sandy, slave of Langdon Chevis BEA 2
Sandy, slave of Uriah Inabnit EDG 18
Sandy, slave of D. C. Tomkins EDG 6
Santacuna, slave SUM 7

Santee Canal Company, slaves of CHA 13
Sara, slave MBO 4
Sarah, slave AND 3
Sarah, slave BAR 10
Sarah, slave BAR 1
Sarah, slave BAR 1
Sarah, slave BAR 13
Sarah, slave BAR 14
Sary, slave BEA 11
Sarah, slave BEA 12
Sarah, slave CHA 12
Sarah, slave COL 5
Sarah, slave COL 9
Sarah, slave COL 11
Sarah, slave DAR 1
Sarah, slave DAR 4
Sarah, slave FAI 2
Sarah, slave FAI 7
Sarah, slave FAI 7
Sarah, slave GRE 2
Sarah, slave GRE 2
Sarah, slave GRE 3
Sarah, slave GRE 3
Sarah, slave GRE 5
Sarah, slave GRE 6
Sarah, slave LAN 2
Sarah, slave LAN 3
Sarah, slave LAN 4
Sarah, slave NEW 1
Sarah, slave NEW 2
Sarah, slave NEW 3
Sarah, slave NEW 4
Sarah, slave NEW 8
Sarah, slave NEW 8
Sarah, slave NEW 10
Sarah, slave ORA 2
Sarah, slave SPA 1
Sarah, slave SUM 2
Sarah, slave SUM 4
Sarah, slave SUM 7
Sarah, slave UNI 4
Sarah, slave WIL 3
Sarah, slave of J. S. Chipley EDG 9
Sarah, slave of W. H. Clement AND 1
Sarah, slave of C. C. Dubose CHA 13
Sarah, slave of P. Gibert ABB 12
Sarah, slave of P. O. Hawthorne ABB 12
Sarah, slave of E. Hill FAI 6
Sarah, slave of J. Holland ABB 19
Sarah, slave of J. Sall ABB 18
Sarah, slave of Elisha Stevens EDG 7
Sarah, slave of Willis Stone EDG 18
Sarah, slave of J. Sturkey EDG 4
Sary, slave of John Swofford PIC 6
Sarah, slave of E. Wagner CHA 6
Sarah, slave of R. M. White ABB 11
Sarah, slave of A. F. Wimbish ABB 13
Sartor, D. R., slaves of UNI 1
Sartor, Rebecca, slave of UNI 1
Sartor, W., slave of UNI 1
Sary, slave COL 3
Sary, slave COL 8
Sass, slave of G. C. Mayson EDG 4
Sassard, John H. CHA 18
Satcher, James R. EDG 18
Satterfield, Asberry PIC 2
Satterfield, HiramPIC 2
Sauls, Ellen J. COL 8
Sauls, Susan E. BEA 14
Saunders, Delia SUM 2
Saunders, Thos E. SUM 2
Sauney, slave BEA 11
Saungdon, slave SUM 13
Savage, Jane (free mulatto) CHA 27
Savage, Jane GRE 3
Savage, Joseph (free mulatto) CHA 27
Savannah, slave of J. Watson ABB 10
Sawyer, Elizabeth AND 7
Sawyer, Mary ORA 4
Sawyer, slave of Wm. Sinkler CHA 3
Saxon, Joshua, slave LAU 4
Saylor, Elizabeth YRK 2
Scaife, F., slaves of UNI 1
Scarborough, Margaret P. SUM 3
Scely, slave ORA 7
Schwerin, Jacob CHA 26
Schine, Michael CHA 20
Scinda, slave WIL 1
Scinda, slave WIL 3
Scinda, slave WIL 5
Scipio, slave FAI 6
Scipio, slave of Dr. Gaillard CHA 1
Scinda, slave of Wm. Sinkler CHA 3
Scipio, slave of Mrs. S. Warings Est. CHA 2
Scooly, Samuel L. YRK 1
Scott, Elizabeth ABB 3
Scott, John CHA 6
Scott, Lawson ABB 13
Scott, Martha AND 2
Scott, Martin CHA 15
Scott, Mary YRK 1
Scott, Morgan CHA 15
Scott, Robert CHA 23
Scott, Samuel H. RIC 2
Scott, Susan J. SUM 12
Scott, Wm. KER 5
Scott, slave MBO 2
Scott, Robert, slave BEA 6
Scott, Tom, slave RIC 3
Scott, William, slave BEA 6
Scott, J. C., slave of ABB 4
Scott, W. C., slave of ABB 3
Scott, slave of Mary Maynad EDG 10
Scriven, Dr. J. P., slaves of BEA 2
Scruggs, John SPA 4
Scruggs, Nancy LAU 9
Scurry, M. H., slave of EDG 10
Scylla, slave of Capt. Robertson CHA 2
Seab, slave LAN 1
Sease, Charles BAR 1
Seawright, John ABB 14
Searle, Ellington, slave of EDG 13
Searle, Marcillas EDG 13
Searle, Richard, slave of EDG 13
Seflers, Sarah HOR 1
Seigling, Ben, slave CHA 20
Seigler, Nancy S. A. EDG 19
Selah, slave BAR 13
Selana, H., slave of CHA 6
Sely, slave of J. Aiken ABB 7
Sele, slave of M. Mays ABB 18
Selenaor, slave ORA 8
Selee, John, slave of LAU 4
Self, Martha EDG 4
Selina, slave COL 1
Seline, slave UNI 6
Sellars, Lavinia CFD 3
Selzer, Mary CHA 24
Semple, Anny EDG 3
Senah, slave of Dr. Nicholson EDG 8
Senet, Margaret CHA 26
Senida, slave COL 4
Senna, slave COL 4
Sephus, slave UNI 6
Serena, slave COL 2
Serena, slave of J. C. Calhoun ABB 13
Serena, slave of Robert N. Hicks CFD 2
Serenah, slave SUM 7
Settle, Sarah EDG 4
Setzler, Martin NEW 8
Severance, E. DAR 3
Sewell, slave of Wm. A. Carson CHA 1
Shadwell, slave GEO 2
Shanklin, J. U., slave of AND 7
Shanklin, Joseph, slaves of PIC 5
Shannon, Sally, slave KER 1
Shans, Thos L., slave of EDG 16
Sharp, R. C., slaves of ABB 12
Sharp, Susannah UNI 6
Sharlot, slave of Tennent CHA 12
Sharper, slave COL 7
Sharper, slave SPA 1
Sharpton, Alex., slaves of EDG 15
Sharpton, Luke BAR 10
Sharpton, Wm. EDG 13
Shaver, George EDG 9
Shaw, Mary LAU 8
Shay, Frances CHA 25
Sheely, Andrew Sen, slave LEX 2
Sheldon, Wm. B., slave of LAU 2

Snell, Margaret, slave LAU 4
Shelor, Jos. R., slave of PIC 6
Shelton, Lewis L. E. EDG 2
Shelton, Wm. J., slave of FAI 5
Shepherd, slave MBO 1
Sheppard, Elizabeth NEW 5
Sheppard, Leither EDG 19
Sheppard, Lewis NEW 6
Sheppard, Wade H. ABB 17
Sheriff, Juggy PIC 1
Shirley, Nathaniel ABB 14
Shirley, N. Est., slave of ABB 14
Shirrards, Wm., slave of AND 5
Shiver, Sarah RIC 1
Shlager, Henry CHA 22
Shocke, slave of James Gregorie CHA 6
Shockly, Mahulday GRE 3
Shoolbred, slave of CHA 10
Shoulbred, Mr., slave of CHA 7
Shropshire, M., slave KER 2
Shuler, Elizabeth ORA 6
Shuler, William ORA 3
Shuler, Wm ORA 1
Shumate, James, slave of AND 2
Shumpert, William ABB 6
Siau, Mary HOR 1
Sibert, G., slaves of ABB 1
Sibla, slave NEW 1
Sibley, E. R. CHR 1
Siddell, A. S. Y., slave of AND 9
Sidney, slave NEW 10
Sidney, slave SUM 6
Sidney, slave WIL 4
Sidney, slave WIL 3
Sike, slave BAR 8
Silas, slave NEW 1
Silas, slave NEW 2
Silas, slave WIL 1
Silena, slave ORA 3
Silla, slave BAR 11
Sillar, slave FAI 7
Sillar, slave of F. W. Pickens EDG 8
Siller, slave LAN 3
Sillera, slave SUM 12
Silly, slave of Thomas P. Ravenel CHA 2
Silus, slave of S. B. Brooks ABB 11
Silvia, slave of J. T. Allen ABB 13
Silvia, slave of John Blakeney CFD 3
Silvia, slave of W. Jowers CFD 1
Silva, slave of James O. Lewis PIC 5
Silvia, slave of J. Watson ABB 10
Silvia, slave MRN 1
Silvy, slave SUM 3
Simeon, slave COL 8
Simeon, slave NEW 2
Simion, slave of Elizabeth Sullivan EDG 15
Simmes, K. Sr., slaves of CHA 1
Simmon, C. H., slave of AND 8
Simmons, Catharine LAU 8
Simmons, David COL 8
Simmons, James, slaves of AND 8
Simmons, John ABB 6
Simmons, John LAU 4
Simmons, Joseph P., slave of LAU 3
Simmons, Mary COL 8
Simon, Elizabeth CHA 15
Simon, slave BAR 1
Simon, slave BAR 9
Simon, slave CHA 10
Simon, slave ORA 6
Simon, slave ORA 8
Simon, slave SUM 9
Simon, slave SUM 10
Simon, slave of Henry Foshee LAU 1
Simon, slave of G. Graves ABB 13
Simon, slave of Elbert Jevore EDG 9
Simons, Joseph GEO 9
Simps, slave of James Ataway EDG 4
Simpson, Amanda AND 6
Simpson, David AND 9
Simpson, John LAU 2
Simpson, J. M. AND 8
Simpson, Margaret R. AND 3
Simpson, Robert ABB 13
Simpson, D., slave of AND 9
Simpson, Rebecca, slaves of PIC 6
Simpson, John T., slave of EDG 10
Simpson, W., slave of FAI 5
Simpson, John W., slave of LAU 3
Sims, J. DAR 2
Sims, Jacob PIC 6
Sims, Nancy LAN 3
Sims, William T. LAU 2
Sims, slave NEW 10
Sims, C. S., slaves of UNI 1
Sina, slave NEW 3
Singleton, Harriet SUM 8
Singelton, infant slaves RIC 2
Singleton, Rebecca SUM 5
Sinia, slave of S. Stevens EDG 7
Sinklair, Archd. MRN 2
Sinkler, Wm., slaves of CHA 3
Sinthia, slave GRE 6
Sippie, slave COL 9
Sippy, slave SPA 4
Sissy, slave of J. C. Raysor ABB 12
Sistair, E. LAN 3
Sites, R., slave of ABB 1
Sitgreaves, A. M. YRK 4
Sitton, Wm., slave of AND 2
Sizemore, Reuben BAR 10
Sizemore, Suckey BAR 10
Skelton, George S. AND 9
Skelton, W. John PIC 6
Skipper, Eliza AND 8
Skipper, Emaline HOR 3
Skipper, John HOR 2
Skren(?), Benja., slaves of EDG 9
Slater, Catherine BAR 1
Sleedly, Julia BAR 1
Sligh, Eugenia NEW 4
Sligh, James S. NEW 1
Sligh, Mary NEW 9
Sloan, J. B., slave of AND 5
Sloan, Thos M. AND 8
Slone, B. F., slaves of AND 4
Smart, slave CHA 10
Smith, slave of John Jenings EDG 19
Smith, infant AND 3
Smith, infant BAR 8
Smith, A., slave of AND 7
Smith, Allen CHA 12
Smith, Bery SPA 3
Smith, C., slaves of ABB 16
Smith, C. L. GRE 6
Smith, Carl W CHA 15
Smith, Caroline CHA 22
Smith, Catharine E. CHA 27
Smith, Charles B. LAU 5
Smith, Charlotte GRE 3
Smith, Chloe, slave BEA 6
Smith, Colmon HOR 1
Smith, E., family of EDG 12
Smith, Elizabeth PIC 2
Smith, Elizabeth ABB 5
Smith, Hannah CHA 23
Smith, Hazel B. YRK 2
Smith, Henry SPA 3
Smith, Henry J. SUM 11
Smith, J., slave of ABB 16
Smith, J. B. CHR 2
Smith, J. Pringle, slaves of BEA 5
Smith, Jacob B., slave of EDG 18
Smith, James GRE 6
Smith, James CHA 12
Smith, James CHA 23
Smith, James AND 7
Smith, James P., slave LEX 1
Smith, Jane, slave of FAI 1
Smith, Joel ABB 9
Smith, John LAU 4
Smith, John HOR 1
Smith, John, slaves of LAU 3
Smith, John B. EDG 1
Smith, John D. RIC 1
Smith, Joshua, slave RIC 1
Smith, Juft HOR 1
Smith, L., slave of ABB 9

Smith, L. A. AND 8
Smith, Lea, slave of FAI 1
Smith, Louisa E. GRE 1
Smith, M., slaves of ABB 16
Smith, Martha MBO 3
Smith, Martha (free mulatto) CHA 26
Smith, Mary LAU 2
Smith, Miray, slave CHA 20
Smith, R., slave of UNI 2
Smith, R. Estate, slaves of BEA 4
Smith, Saml, slave BEA 6
Smith, Saml. J. EDG 12
Smith, Stephen R. MRN 1
Smith, Thomas ABB 16
Smith, Thomas, slaves LEX 1
Smith, Thos PIC 2
Smith, W., slave of ABB 9
Smith, W. R., slave of LAU 1
Smoke, Ginsey BAR 1
Smyly, D. C., slave of EDG 3
Snow, Bethany LAU 3
Sol, slave BAR 8
Sol, slave of William J. Wightman EDG 17
Solomon, slave COL 8
Solomon, slave of William T. Gardner EDG 14
Sophia, slave GEO 3
Sopha, slave YRK 2
Sophia, slave of Joseph Adams EDG 17
Sophia, slave of Sarah B. Jones ABB 1
Sophy, slave of J. Venning CHA 7
Soue, slave of E. Dubose CHA 3
Southerland, Eliza, slave PIC 3
Southerland, Paschal PIC 3
Southerland, Wm., slave PIC 3
Sowell, Elizh. KER 3
Sox, Martin LEX 1
Spann, Caroline SUM 10
Spann, H. R., family of EDG 11
Spann, H. R. (JAILOR) EDG 11
Spann, James SUM 9
Spear, Robt H. GRE 8
Spearman, Thomas, slave of LAU 1
Spears, Andrew LAU 5
Spears, Wm MBO 1
Speer, J., slave of ABB 13
Speer, J. M., slave of ABB 13
Spence, Charles ABB 7
Spence, Josephine ABB 1
Spencer, slave of J. Lifford ABB 7
Spencer, slave of C. Smith ABB 16
Spencer, Amanda UNI 5
Spencer, Eliza BAR 6
Spencer, Harriet UNI 6
Spires, Henry, slave of EDG 2
Spivey, Eli HOR 3
Spranchen, Claus CHA 18
Spray, Elizabeth YRK 2
Sproul, E., slave of ABB 9
Sproull, R., slaves of ABB 18
Sproull, Samuel M. ABB 18
Squire, slave NEW 9
Squire, slave UNI 5
St. Amand, Francis CHA 17
St. John, Nancy UNI 4
Stabler, Henry ORA 9
Stafford, John CFD 2
Stafford, Sarah CFD 2
Stallings, Eliza BAR 4
Stallings, Jesse BAR 8
Stallings, Susannah BAR 5
Stallworth, Amos, slave of EDG 9
Stalmaker, Seloin, slave of EDG 9
Stalmaker, E. B. EDG 9
Stalmaker, M. E. EDG 9
Stanley, Mary COL 1
Stanridge, Henrietta PIC 6
Stanridge, Mary PIC 6
Stanton, Alex. MOB 1
Starkman, Anna CHA 23
Steedman, Walter C. YRK 2
Steele, James, slave of AND 7
Steele, Mary Jane CFD 2
Steen, D., slave of UNI 2
Stelling, Henry CHA 22
Stepfader, William CHA 24
Stephen, slave BAR 2
Stephen, slave GEO 2
Stephen, slave HOR 2
Stephen, slave NEW 3
Stephen, slave NEW 5
Stephen, slave NEW 10
Stephen, slave SUM 6
Stephen, slave WIL 1
Stephen, slave of N. Calhoun ABB 19
Stephen, slave of J. Cason FAI 1
Stephen, slave of Mrs. Rutledge CHA 11
Stephens, David AND 8
Stephens, Sarah CHA 16
Stephenson, John, slave of AND 9
Stepney, slave BAR 1
Stepney, slave ORA 2
Sterling, Samuel, slave of FAI 3
Stevens, S., slave of EDG 7
Stevens, Elisha, slaves of EDG 7
Stevens, Henry L., slaves of CHA 2
Stevens, E. S. CHA 16
Stevenson, Francis W. FAI 3
Stevenson, John ABB 15
Stevenson, J. A., slaves of UNI 2
Steverson, James C. ORA 2
Stewart, Rebecca EDG 19
Stewart, Peter T. ABB 19
Stewart, Martha CHR 1
Stewart, Lincoln YRK 2
Stewart, John CHR 2
Stewart, Ellen N. YRK 2
Still, E., slave of EDG 7
Still, James, family of EDG 12
Still, James Jr. EDG 12
Still, Martha BAR 4
Still, Robert FAI 7
Still, Sarah FAI 7
Still, Temperance EDG 7
Stinemetz, Amy, slave CFD 2
Stingmaker, John, slave of EDG 14
Stinson, Wm. A. AND 5
Stockman, John CHA 26
Stoddard, Obadiah CHA 23
Stokes, J. W., slave of EDG 2
Stokes, James BAR 14
Stokes, Julia BAR 1
Stokes, Margaret SUM 6
Stokes, Rachel BAR 1
Stokes, Sarah A. EDG 4
Stone, Dempsey, slave of BEA 1
Stone, Willis, slave of EDG 18
Stone, David B. PIC 6
Stone, Elijah ORA 2
Stone, Elizabeth AND 1
Stone, Henry MRN 1
Stone, Jefferson GRE 6
Stone, John D. NEW 9
Stone, Margaret ABB 14
Stone, Mariah PIC 1
Stone, Richard EDG 13
Stone, Virgil WIL 3
Stoney, slave BAR 12
Storm, David CHA 23
Story, Ann LAN 4
Strain, Archibald CHR 2
Strain, Elizabeth CHR 2
Strains, Mary, slave of EDG 1
Strange, Colclough B. SUM 2
Strapon, slave COL 9
Stratford, Nancy, slave KER 1
Stratford, Phillip, slave KER 1
Strawder, Eliza M. NEW 5
Strawder, Eliza M. NEW 7
Strawther, Reubin (free black) ABB 2
Streeter, Elesia CFD 3
Stribbling, Elizabeth PIC 5
Stribling, Sophronia AND 8
Stribbling, M. Stokes PIC 6
Striclan, Elizabeth ABB 8
Strohecker, John L. CHA 12
Strong, James CHR 2
Strother, N. M., slave of ABB 5

Strowd, Aggy EDG 12
Strowd, Elizabeth EDG 12
Strowd, Sarah EDG 12
Stuart, Mrs. M. B., slaves of BEA 15
Stuart, Minty, slave BEA 9
Stuart, Rinah, slave BEA 9
Stuckey, Addison SUM 9
Sturges, Amelia J. YRK 1
Sturges, Barbra YRK 1
Sturges, Jane YRK 2
Sturges, Susan YRK 1
Sturkey, J., slave of EDG 4
Stuckey, J. DAR 3
Suber, John NEW 5
Suck, slave of CFD 3
Willis Alsobrook
Suckey, slave BAR 1
Suckey, slave DAR 2
Suckey, slave YRK 3
Suckey, slave of M. L. Grasty EDG 2
Suckey, slave of Richard Searle EDG 13
Sue, slave GEO 3
Sue, slave DAR 3
Sue, slave DAR 2
Sue, slave GEO 7
Sue, slave GEO 8
Sue, slave GEO 4
Sue, slave of Keating Ball CHA 2
Sue, slave of T. W. Porcher CHA 3
Sue, slave of Hugh Rose BEA 2
Sue, slave of John S.White CHA 1
Suggs, Jonas HOR 3
Sukey, slave ORA 5
Sukey, slave CHA 5
Sukey, slave BAR 2
Sukey, slave of Miss H. GaillardCHA 3
Sukey, slave of S. S. Palmer CHA 9
Sullivan, Anna B. AND 5
Sullivan, Calvin CFD 3
Sullivan, Eliza-beth, slaves of EDG 15
Sullivan, Joseph LAU 8
Sullivan, Oscar BAR 12
Sullivan, Robert BAR 12
Sullivan, Robert, slave of LAU 7
Summer(?), slave WIL 2
Summer, slave SUM 1
Summer, Joseph P., slave LEX 2
Summer, Thomas N. NEW 2
Summer, Thomas N. NEW 6
Summers, Jno COL 5
Suno, slave SUM 5
Surtis, T. W. CHA 21
Susan, slave BAR 12
Susan, slave UNI 4
Susan, slave ORA 8
Susan, slave BAR 7
Susan, slave of W. Breazeal AND 3
Susan, slave WIL 2
Susan, slave COL 1
Susan, slave SUM 4
Susan, slave SUM 6
Susan, slave SPA 1
Susan, slave DAR 4
Susan, slave BEA 12
Susan, slave of BEA 2
Benjamin F. Buckner
Susan, slave SUM 5
Susan, slave SUM 9
Susan, slave SUM 5
Susan, slave SUM 10
Susan, slave of Wm. Garrett EDG 16
Susan, slave of Wm. Garrett EDG 15
Susan, slave of C. Jones EDG 11
Susan, slave of W. McCants CHA 6
Susan, slave of T. E. Padget EDG 6
Susan, slave of D. C. Smyly EDG 3
Susanah, slave SUM 3
Susanna, slave COL 3
Susannah, slave SUM 9
Susanna, slave NEW 7
Susannah, slave SUM 12
Susannah, slave SPA 4
Susannah, slave of J. Fair ABB 15
Susannah, slave of J. S. Reid ABB 5
Susy, slave WIL 1
Sutton, Ellen CHA 26
Sutton, William CHA 26
Suzy, slave CHA 10
Syfrett, Elizabeth ORA 6
Syfrett, Frederick ORA 6
Sylla, slave DAR 2
Sylva, slave ORA 4
Sylva, slave ORA 1
Sylva, slave GRE 8
Sylvia, slave GRE 1
Sylvia, slave COL 2
Sylvia, slave COL 3
Sylvia, slave GEO 2
Sylvia, slave BAR 9
Sylvia, slave of Langdon Chevis BEA 2
Sylvia, slave of BEA 1
Dr. William C. Daniels
Sylvy, slave WIL 3
Sylvy, slave WIL 4
Symmes, F. W., slave of AND 7
Symmes, George W. AND 4
Syrus, slave of Jonothan Tayler EDG 15
Swails, James MRN 1
Swan, Timothy FAI 3
Sweat, Thomas J. CFD 2
Sweegan, Matthew CHA 22
Swofford, John, slave PIC 6
Swygert, Jacob, slave LEX 2
Swygert, Sanders, slave LEX 1

Tacer, slave of A. McClellan CHA 9
Tagar, slave COL 1
Takes(?), Elias, slave of EDG 9
Talbert, B., slave of ABB 1
Talbert, Mary E. EDG 1
Talbert, R. M., slave of EDG 1
Talbird, Cynthia, slave BEA 9
Talbert, Jos A., slave of EDG 17
Talitha, slave of Sally Miles EDG 3
Tallman, M. C., slaves of ABB 4
Tamar, slave NEW 10
Tamar, slave BAR 12
Tanner, Thomas MRN 1
Tanner, William MRN 1
Tannon, slave CHA 10
Tarleton, slave of John Coleman EDG 19
Tarn, slave of John Tompkins EDG 17
Tarplet, Joel CHR 4
Tarsey, slave LAN 4
Tate, A. ORA 2
Tayler, Jonothan, slaves of EDG 15
Tayler, Lewis CHA 4
Tayler, Wesley CHA 4
Taylor, slave BAR 12
Taylor, D. S., slaves of AND 6
Taylor, Elizh. KER 3
Taylor, G. P. LAN 3
Taylor, Jacob LEX 3
Taylor, Lavinia NEW 10
Taylor, Lucy J. ABB 17
Taylor, Martha MRN 1
Taylor, Mary NEW 10
Taylor, Nancy GRE 4
Taylor, Robert CHA 16
Taylor, Rose, slave RIC 3
Taylor, S., slave KER 3
Taylor, Sarah, slave LEX 4
Taylor, Tenah, slave RIC 3
Taylor, W. J., slaves of ABB 4
Teague, Elijah, slave of AND 7
Teague, Thomas, slave of LAU 1
Telford, ArtimisiaAND 2
Templeton, James D. ABB 17
Templeton, W., slaves of ABB 17
Tena, slave NEW 1
Tena, slave ORA 2
Tena, slave FAI 6
Tenah, slave LAN 2
Tenah, slave of James Blackwell EDG 11
Tenah, slave of S. Johnson ABB 13
Tenah, slave of R. Laurens CHA 7
Tenant, January, slave CHA 21
Tenant, Gilbert, slave of EDG 15
Tenas, slave SUM 13
Tennant, James SUM 2
Tennant, Rachel A. SUM 1
Tennant, W., slaves of CHA 3

Tennant, W.,
slave of ABB 3
Tennet, slave of CHA 12
Tenny, slave of CHA 2
Henry L. Stevens
Teresa, slave BEA 14
Teresa, slave of
W. P. Brooks ABB 10
Tersa, slave LAN 4
Terry, John,
slave of EDG 4
Thames, Vermele SUM 1
Tharin, Caroline CHA 25
Thelford, Ann CHA 18
Theophilus, Thomas
CHA 27
Thisby, slave of
John S. White CHA 1
Thom, slave of
Thos Hill EDG 18
Thomas, slave BAR 9
Thomas, slave GEO 5
Thomas, slave GEO 2
Thomas, slave COL 6
Thomas,slave SUM 6
Thomas, slave SUM 7
Thomas, slave NEW 5
Thomas, slave NEW 5
Thomas, slave NEW 3
Thomas, slave NEW 10
Thomas, slave SUM 12
Thomas, slave LAN 4
Thomas, slave LAN 3
Thomas, slave GRE 8
Thomas, slave GRE 7
Thomas, slave(?) GRE 4
Thos, slave COL 7
Thos, slave SUM 13
Thos, slave BAR 13
Thomas, slave of
F. Mims EDG 11
Thomas, slave of
A. Tittle ABB 2
Thomas, slave of
S. E. Waring FAI 8
Thomas, Amelia,
slave CHA 27
Thomas, Caroline MBO 1
Thomas, Eliza BEA 14
Thomas, Jas.,
slave of UNI 1
Thomas, Laundace ORA 2
Thomas, Maria KER 3
Thomas, Mary
(free black) CHA 27
Thomas, Reuben,
slave of LAU 6
Thomas, Thomas PIC 6
Thomas, W.,
slave of FAI 8
Thomas, W.,
slave of UNI 1
Thomasiner, slave DAR 1
Thomason, George LAU 8
Thomason, James
C., slave YRK 5
Thomoson, Jonas LAU 8
Thompson, slave
of G. W. Lomas ABB 16
Thompson, Ann ORA 6
Thompson, Eliza ORA 6
Thompson, Eliza-
beth ABB 18
Thompson, Eliot LAU 3
Thompson, John AND 6
Thompson, Joseph GRE 4
Thompson, Marshal EDG 8

Thompson, Nancy LAU 1
Thompson, T.,
slaves of ABB 5
Thompson, Waddy,
slaves of EDG 8
Thomson, Henry NEW 5
Thomson, John UNI 4
Thomson, Warwick,
slave BEA 6
Thorn, W.,
slave of FAI 8
Threatt, Raney CFD 3
Thurman, John,
slaves of EDG 14
Thurmond, William,
slave of EDG 1
Tidwell, S.,
slaves of FAI 1
Tiedman, Adaline CHA 25
Tilda, slave FAI 7
Tiller, slave of
J. E. G. Bell ABB 13
Tillman, B. R. EDG 6
Tillman, J. LAN 4
Tillman, Mrs. S.
A., family of EDG 6
Tillman, Tabitha,
slave of EDG 16
Tilly, slave LAN 2
Tilman, slave of
E. Mattison ABB 14
Tim, slave COL 7
Timmerman, John
Allan EDG 5
Timmerman, M.,
family of EDG 5
Timmerman, Peter EDG 5
Timmerman, R.,
family EDG 5
Tina, slave SUM 10
Tinah, slave COL 6
Tinah, slave CHA 10
Tincker , John CHA 23
Tiner, slave SUM 11
Tisby, slave of
J. M. Speer ABB 13
Tisdale, Mary J. WIL 4
Tisdale, Susan T.WIL 5
Tittle, A.,
slave of ABB 2
Tittle, Anthony ABB 2
Tittle, Robert ABB 2
Titus, slave of CHA 3
James Gaillard Sr.
Tobithia, slave YRK 4
Toby, slave GEO 6
Toby, slave GEO 2
Toby, slave COL 1
Toby, slave of
S. Dubose CHA 2
Todd, E.,
slave of ABB 18
Todd, John,
slave of LAU 1
Todd, Jonas R.,
slaves of LAU 5
Todd, Samuel N.,
slave of LAU 3
Todd, W. H. L. HOR 2
Tolson, M. DAR 2
Tom, slave BAR 10
Tom, slave BAR 11
Tom, slave BAR 7
Tom, slave BAR 1
Tom, slave BAR 13
Tom, slave CHA 12
Tom, slave DAR 3

Tom, slave ORA 9
Tom, slave ORA 8
Tom, slave YRK 3
Tom, slave MRN 3
Tom, slave MBO 2
Tom, slave COL 12
Tom, slave UNI 8
Tom, slave COL 12
Tom, slave GEO 5
Tom, slave SUM 5
Tom, slave SUM 8
Tom, slave SUM 6
Tom, slave BEA 13
Tom, slave of
J. C. Ball CHA 2
Tom, slave of
Keating Ball CHA 2
Tom, slave of
S. Barksdale ABB 2
Tom, slave of
D. Calhoun ABB 19
Tom, slave of
W. T. Drennan ABB 3
Tom, slave of
F. H. Edington FAI 3
Tom, slave of
D. & L. FranklinABB 15
Tom, slave of BEA 1
Capt. Nathan Johnson
Tom, slave of
Felix Lake EDG 6
Tom, slave of
Joseph M. LawtonBEA 1
Tom, slave of
T. J. Legare CHA 6
Tom, slave of
J. .F. Marshal ABB 6
Tom, slave of
James B. Mobley FAI 6
Tom, slave of
Saml Porcher CHA 13
Tom, slave of
Elias Takes EDG 9
Tom, slave of
R. Watson ABB 10
Tommy, slave GEO 3
Tommy, slave of CHA 13
Mrs. R. J. Couturier
Tomlinson, H. M.,
slaves of CFD 2
Tompkins, D. C.,
slave of EDG 6
Tompkins, John,
slaves of EDG 17
Tomtry, slave GEO 1
Tony, slave LAN 1
Toney, slave SUM 5
Tony, slave MRN 2
Tony, slave of
Nancy Delaughter EDG 15
Tony, slave of
S. Wideman ABB 4
Tony, Margaret ORA 4
Tool, A.,
slave of CHA 9
Tooley, Clarance CHA 17
Toomer,A. N. Dr.,
slaves of CHA 6
Toomer, N. L.,
slave of CHA 6
Tooty, slave CHA 10
Torbert, S. J. KER 3
Toore, Adaline CHA 22
Touchstone, infant BAR 10
Towles, Elizabeth EDG 1
Towles, O.,
slaves of EDG 7

Name	County	No.
Towns, Henry H.	ABB	3
Travis, slave	MRN	2
Traylor, A. J., slaves of	EDG	10
Trecy, slave	ORA	9
Trewerks, Mary	MRN	2
Tribble, Terril A.	ABB	7
Trotter, Josiah	PIC	4
Trotter, Wm.	EDG	7
Truesdell, Frances	KER	2
Truesdell, Penny, slave	KER	2
Trussel, Posey, slaves of	AND	1
Tucker, slave	GRE	6
Tucker, Atticus, slaves of	EDG	4
Tucker, John	BAR	13
Tudor, Elizabeth	WIL	2
Tuggers, Daniel	CHA	17
Tullis, Margaret E.	ABB	3
Tully, slave of Wm. Ducass	CHA	9
Tunno, slave	BAR	2
Tupper, Lucy J.	CHA	16
Turnage, William	CFD	2
Turnbull, J. S., slave of	ABB	4
Turner, ___(?)	KER	3
Turner, Albert, family of	EDG	12
Turner, Benjamin	GRE	4
Turner, Bluet	EDG	18
Turner, Emanuel, slave	PIC	4
Turner, Felix S.	PIC	2
Turner, H. C., family of	EDG	5
Turner, James A.	EDG	9
Turner, Jane, slaves of	EDG	9
Turner, John	BAR	9
Turner, Mary	EDG	12
Turner Oliver	CHR	5
Turner, William	LAU	6
Turnipseed, Elizabeth	NEW	7
Turnipseed, Sarah J.	NEW	7
Tyler, Charlotte	CHA	17
Tyler, Lucia	BAR	5
Tyra, slave	BEA	13
Tyra, slave	BEA	11
Tyra, slave	COL	9
Tyler, slave of B. E. Belcher	ABB	4
Urt, Henry	CHA	22
Usery, Amanda	BAR	7
Usher, Mary	MBO	2
Vance, A., slaves of	ABB	11
Vance, David, slave of	LAU	3
Vance, J., slaves of	ABB	17
Vansant, Nancy	LEX	3
Vansant, Walter	LEX	3
Varn, Rosina	BAR	1
Varnadere, Suckey	BEA	1
Varnerdore, James	BEA	1
Varnadore, Moses	BEA	1
Vaughan, Charlotte	KER	1
Vaughan, Elizh.	KER	1
Vaughan, John	KER	1
Vaughan, Judy	KER	1
Vaughn, Morris	GRE	6
Vaughan, Russel, slave of	EDG	9
Vaun(?), Ann H.	SUM	2
Venning, J., slaves of	CHA	7
Venters, Alexander	WIL	3
Venus, slave	SUM	9
Venus, slave	GEO	8
Venus, slave	WIL	1
Venus, slave	COL	7
Venus, slave	ORA	4
Venus, slave	SUM	12
Venus, slave of J. B. Bull	ABB	2
Venus, slave of Wm. Ducass	CHA	9
Verner, Rebecca	PIC	6
Verner, Wooley	CHA	22
Vester, slave	SUM	1
Vickory, H. A.	PIC	4
Vicory, F.	LAN	4
Vicory, O.	LAN	1
Vicory, O.	LAN	2
Vilett, slave	WIL	3
Villeponteaux, Mr., slave of	CHA	4
Villeponteaux, W. D., slave of	CHA	13
Willines, Jas.	LAN	3
Villines, W.	LAN	3
Vina, slave	ORA	5
Vincent, slave	FAI	3
Vincent, slave of J. M. Chiles	ABB	1
Viney, slave of Joseph Rearden	EDG	12
Viney, slave of R. M. White	ABB	11
Viny, slave of Mrs. Ladd	FAI	6
Violet, slave	SUM	13
Violet, slave	SUM	8
Violet, slave of Milley Chapman	CFD	1
Virgil, slave	WIL	2
Virginia, slave	BEA	11
Vogel, Joe, slave	CHA	25
Von Glahn, Hannah	CHA	20
Vooer, Hertenza	CHA	26
Voorhand, Charles E.	CHA	17
Waddell, J. C.	SPA	3
Waddill, Edmund	GRE	5
Wade, slave	ORA	1
Wade, slave of D. New	ABB	1
Wade, Edward, slave of	LAU	1
Wadkins, Samuel	PIC	6
Wadsworth, Elisa, slave	NEW	1
Wadsworth, Mary A., slave	NEW	1
Wadsworth, R.	DAR	4
Wages, Mary J.	FAI	3
Wages, Saml	CHR	3
Wagner, E., slave of	CHA	6
Wagner, Thusnald	CHA	20
Waites, John M.	EDG	7
Waits, Alley	EDG	19
Waits, Phillip, slave of	LAU	8
Waldrep, Smith	GRE	5
Walker, Alexander, slave of	EDG	17
Walker, Ann M.	ABB	2
Walker, Georgiana Frances	EDG	6
Walker, J.	ORA	4
Walker, Margaret	BAR	6
Walker, Mary	GRE	6
Walker, R., slaves of	ABB	3
Walker, Teresa	BAR	6
Walker, William, slaves of	EDG	15
Walker, Z., slave of	EDG	4
Wall, Missouri	BAR	9
Wall, Nancy	SPA	1
Wall, Robt	SPA	4
Wallace, slave	MBO	2
Wallace, slave	BAR	2
Wallace, Daniel	LAU	3
Wallace, Henry	CFD	2
Wallace, M. M.	AND	6
Wallace, Rubin	HOR	3
Wallen, Maria T.	AND	6
Waller, Benj. F.	ABB	11
Walling, W. W., slaves of	EDG	2
Walsor, John	NEW	9
Walter, slave	NEW	7
Walter, slave	YRK	4
Walter, slave	NEW	1
Walter, Elias E.	CHA	25
Walters, Nancy	WIL	5
Wansey, slave of D. C. Tompkins	EDG	6
Ward, slave	NEW	9
Ward, C. J.	EDG	11
Ward, Pamela	LAU	1
Ward, Sarah	GRE	1
Ward, William	GEO	6
Wardlaw, Alice	EDG	11
Wardlaw, D. L., slave of	ABB	6
Wardlaw, F. H., infant of	EDG	11
Ware, Margaret	GRE	2
Ware, Susan W.	EDG	15
Waring, John	FAI	8
Waring, S. E., slaves of	FAI	8
Waring, Dr. M., slaves of	CHA	2
Waring, Mrs. S. Est.	CHA	2
Warley, slave	LAN	4
Warley, Paul	CHA	4
Warren, slave	SUM	3
Warren, slave	SUM	6
Warren, slave of John Clardy	AND	3
Warshaw, John H.	SUM	12
Wash, slave	BAR	14
Wash, slave of M. W. Clary	EDG	4
Wash, Nancy, slave of	EDG	17
Washington, slave	GRE	3
Washington, slave	FAI	7
Washington, slave	NEW	3
Washington, slave	SPA	3
Washington, slave	SUM	10

Washington, slave SUM 7
Washington, slave SUM 13
Washington, slave BAR 2
Wassin, Jno GRE 3
Wat, slave of A. Richey ABB 7
Waters, William MRN 2
Waties, slave SUM 5
Watkins, Briget KER 4
Watkins, Hilary, slave KER 1
Watkins, James E. AND 4
Watkins, Louisa A. KER 4
Watkins, M. E. KER 4
Watkins, Rachael, slave KER 1
Watson, B. H., slave of ABB 17
Watson, Caroline KER 4
Watson,Cynthia L. AND 6
Watson, Daniel, slave of AND 5
Watson, J., slaves of ABB 10
Watson, J., ABB 10
Estate, slaves of
Watson, Mary SUM 5
Watson, Mary SUM 13
Watson, R., slaves of ABB 10
Watson, R. W., slaves of FAI 3
Watson, Sarah PIC 4
Watson, Stanmore, slaves of EDG 18
Watson, Tabitha, slave of EDG 3
Watson, Tilman, slaves of EDG 18
Watson, Wm. KER 4
Watt, slave of John Lipscomb EDG 11
Watt, slave of Nancy Wash EDG 17
Watters(?), Franklin L. YRK 3
Watts, Rebecca GEO 5
Watts, William D., slaves of LAU 2
Wauly, slave BEA 13
Way, Ann EDG 14
Weatherly, Wm MBO 3
Weathers, Susan FAI 6
Weathersbee, Sally BAR 5
Weaver, James (free black) WIL 3
Webear, William, slave YRK 5
Webb, Clayton, slave of AND 7
Webb, Elisha, slave of AND 8
Webb, William, slave of AND 4
Webber, Joseph F. YRK 5
Webster, George MBO 2
Webster, James MBO 2
Weed, Andrew ABB 4
Weeks, Neighbor L. SUM 4
Weeks, Thomas NEW 6
Weir, T., slave of ABB 11
Welberger, Catharine E. CHA 22
Welch, Susan PIC 6
Weldon, John T. SUM 7
Weldone, slave COL 2
Wells, Rebecca SUM 2
Welsh, Elizth SUM 11
Welsh, John LAN 3
Werner, Julius AND 7
Werts, Nancy M. L. EDG 19
Werts, Olive NEW 3
Werts, Thomas S. NEW 4
Wesley, slave SUM 3
Wesley, slave BAR 2
West, slave of R. C. Ritchie ABB 15
West, E. C., slave of EDG 2
Wever, J. R., slave of EDG 3
Whaley, Elizabeth ABB 19
Wharton, Martha H. (free black) ABB 2
Wharton, Wm. M. (free black) ABB 2
Whatley, James B. ABB 16
Whatley, Ransom EDG 7
Whatley, Shirley, slave of EDG 7
Whatley, William EDG 12
Whatly, Perry C. ABB 18
Whelden, Wm., slave of CHA 6
Whisenant, Michel, slave YRK 5
White(?), Elizabeth YRK 1
White, Abner EDG 17
White, Abner D. EDG 8
White, Ellen (free mulatto) CHA 24
White, Eliphu COL 9
White, Henry SUM 2
White, John J. SUM 2
White, John L. ABB 16
White, John S. SPA 1
White, John S., slaves of CHA 1
White, Josiah MRN 1
White, Leonard J. ABB 16
White, Mary EDG 17
White, Mary E. SUM 14
White, R. M., slaves of ABB 11
White, S., slave of CHA 1
White,Thos CHA 4
White, Thomas C. ABB 19
White, Thomas M. AND 8
Whitehead, Louisa SUM 1
Whitesides, B., slave of CHA 6
Whitfield, slave of L. Reynolds ABB 10
Whitfield, slave of R. Watson ABB 10
Whiting, Kate N. CHA 17
Whitlock, W. J. EDG 6
Whitman, James AND 6
Whitman, Margaret YRK 2
Whitman, Tabitha AND 6
Whitman, Wesley AND 6
Whitmore, Thos H. Jr. LAU 6
Whitney, Eliza CHA 17
Whitney, Eliza Ann CHA 21
Whitney, Martha, slave CHA 17
Whitten, Jackson AND 7
Whittle, Mark B., slave of EDG 19
Wiat, slave of L. C. Jeter UNI 2
Wicker, E. E. NEW 2
Wicker, Mary NEW 5
Wideman, J., slaves of ABB 4
Wideman, J. H., slave of ABB 1
Wideman, Jenny K. ABB 4
Wideman, Robert H. ABB 1
Wideman, S., slave of ABB 4
Wideman, Samuel ABB 4
Wideman, Sarah, slave of ABB 1
Wightman, Jane, slave CHA 25
Wightman, William J., slaves of EDG 17
Wikeson, John J. YRK 4
Wilbanks, Charles UNI 8
Wilbanks, Martha UNI 8
Wilcox, John CFD 3
Wiles, Adam J. ORA 3
Wiles, Matilda YRK 1
Wiley, slave SUM 14
Wiley, slave NEW 6
Wiley(?), slave of W. F. Winn EDG 4
Wiley, slave of D. Mobley FAI 8
Wiley, D., slave of ABB 9
Wilkerson, Jno LAN 4
Wilkinson, G. O., slaves of EDG 14
Wilkison, Mary MBO 1
Wilks, John GEO 6
Wilks, Mildred J. CHR 5
Wilks, Whitee LAU 4
Wilks, Whitee, slave of LAU 4
Will, slave COL 11
Will, slave COL 1
Will, slave GEO 3
Will, slave GEO 5
Will, slave BEA 11
Will, slave ORA 5
Will, slave ORA 3
Will, slave SUM 12
Will, slave of K. Simmes Sr. CHA 1
Will, slave of Dempsey Stone BEA 1
Willard, Jane UNI 6
Willborn, slave of J. E. Allen AND 1
William, slave BAR 6
William, slave CHA 10
William, slave WIL 5
William, slave COL 9
William, slave COL 8
William, slave COL 2
William, slave COL 1
William, slave GEO 4
William, slave GEO 6
William, slave MBO 2
William, slave SUM 13
William, slave FAI 6
William, slave ORA 1
William, slave GRE 2
William, slave GRE 4
William, slave GRE 7
William, slave LAN 1
William, slave LAN 4

William, slave UNI 7
William, slave NEW 2
William, slave NEW 10
William, slave ORA 9
William, slave SUM 4
Wm, slave SUM 14
William, slave
of George Addy EDG 19
William, slave
of J. J. BarnetABB 7
William, slave
of G. Bigby ABB 14
William, slave EDG 3
of Thomax Claxton
William, slave
of Dr. William C.
DanielsBEA 1
William, slave EDG 14
of Wiley Glover
William, slave
of Joseph Long EDG 20
William, slave
of R. Maddox ABB 12
William, slave AND 4
of William Ross
William, slave
of Wm Sitton AND 2
William, slave
of Lea Smith FAI 1
William, slave
of W. J. TaylorABB 4
Williams, Batte,
family of EDG 11
Williams, CharlesGRE 8
Williams, David BAR 14
Williams, David
J., slave of LAU 4
Williams, Elmira
L. PIC 2
Williams, George
W. YRK 2
Williams, J. G.,
slave of LAU 1
Williams, Jessee EDG 3
Williams, Jo.,
slave PIC 4
Williams, John CHA 19
Williams, John C.LAU 5
Williams, John D.GRE 5
Williams, John D.,LAU 2
slaves of
Williams, John H. AND 2
Williams, M. J.,
slave of ABB 2
Williams, M. W. SPA 4
Williams, Mary,
slave PIC 4
Williams, Mary A. PIC 2
Williams, Mary J. HOR 3
Williams, Mary S. EDG 11
Williams, Milly LAN 3
Williams, N. M.,
family of EDG 11
Williams, Nancy LEX 3
Williams, Rachael BEA 11
Williams, Sarah C.YRK 2
Williams, W.,
slave of EDG 7
Williams, W. A.,
slave of AND 2
Williamson, M.,
slave of FAI 8
Williamson, S. DAR 1
Williamson, Ster-
ling C., slave LEX 2
Williman, Dicy GRE 1
Willis, slave ORA 4
Willis, slave NEW 8
Willis, slave ORA 1
Willis, slave SUM 10
Willis, slave EDG 9
of T. A. Addison
Willis, slave
of Mary Britt ABB 1
Willis, slave of
S. B. Brooks ABB 11
Willis, slave of
Thomas Gregory UNI 1
Willis, slave of
J. Watson ABB 10
Willis, Charity BAR 4
Willson, slave of
Wm. Mattison AND 1
Willson, James,
slave of AND 3
Willson, Mary J. AND 3
Wilson, slave SUM 8
Wilson, slave SPA 3
Wilson, slave ORA 4
Wilson, slave of
Elijah Gayden FAI 8
Wilson, slave of
Waddy Thompson EDG 8
Wilson & McGowan,
slave of ABB 6
Wilson, Andrew PIC 6
Wilson, Clara NEW 10
Wilson, E. DAR 2
Wilson, E. GEO 6
Wilson, Elizabeth
H. SUM 12
Wilson, Elwin YRK 5
Wilson, George
(free mulatto) GEO 6
Wilson, Green LAU 5
Wilson, James CHA 27
Wilson, James S. ABB 6
Wilson, Jane
(free black) CHA 27
Wilson, Jane M. BEA 10
Wilson, John CHA 4
Wilson, John SUM 9
Wilson, John T. SUM 2
Wilson, L. C.,
slave of ABB 7
Wilson, Mary T. WIL 3
Wilson, R. S. CHR 1
Wilson, Robert YRK 4
Wilson, Sarah A. ABB 6
Wilson, Stephen,
slave of EDG 14
Wilson, W.,
slave of ABB 12
Wilson, Wm. SUM 6
Wilson, Wm. KER 4
Wimbish, A. F.,
slave of ABB 13
Windsor, slave COL 10
Windum, M. CHA 13
Wingard, Michael,
slave LEX 2
Winn, W. F.,
slave of EDG 4
Winney, slave UNI 6
Winney, slave of
J. Durham FAI 8
Winny, slave MBO 1
Winny, slave SPA 4
Winny, slave of
T. C. Haskill ABB 17
Winston, slave of
G. W. Huckale ABB 8
Winters, Matilda AND 5
Winthrop, William,
slave CHA 26
Wisdom, slave of CFD 1
Alexander McQueen
Wise, Eliza EDG 2
Wise, Jane MRN 2
Witt, Margaret R. NEW 4
Wofford, John SPA 1
Wood, Elizabeth BAR 9
Wood, Green SPA 3
Wood, John A. J. YRK 5
Woodberry, D. A. CHA 19
Wooderd, Jeffer-
son LEX 3
Woods, F. DAR 1
Woods, J. DAR 4
Woods, R.,
slave of ABB 14
Woodside, Mary GRE 6
Woodward, Beck,
slave RIC 2
Woodward, Frank,
slave RIC 2
Woodward, Hender-
son, slave RIC 2
Woodward, Henry SUM 6
Woodward, Joe,
slave RIC 2
Woodward, John SUM 6
Woodward, Miles RIC 2
Woodward, Philip,
slave RIC 2
Woodward, Richard FAI 1
Woodward, Sarah,
slave RIC 2
Woodward, William
M., slaves of FAI 5
Woodward, Winney,
slave RIC 2
Wooley, Elsy BAR 4
Woolf, Archable LEX 4
Woolf, Archable,
slaves LEX 4
Workman, James N. YRK 3
Workman, Samuel LAU 2
Workman, Samuel LAU 4
Wragg, Silva,
slave CHA 21
Wright, Cynthia UNI 6
Wright, John CHR 3
Wright, John D.,
slave of LAU 3
Wright, William F.AND 1
Wrights, Mrs. C.,
slave of AND 8
Wylie, William H. YRK 3
Wyms, Ellen CHA 18

Xenophon, slave COL 12

Yaffy, slave COL 1
Yancy, slave of
M. V. Richey ABB 16
Yarber, Julia CFD 1
Yates, Deborah CHA 15
Yates, New,
slave CHA 16
Yates, William CHA 15
Yeadon, Benjamin,
slave CHA 20
Yeargin, Benjamin GRE 1
Yeargin, Jane GRE 2
Yeats, Elith. SUM 8
Yelding, Emily EDG 4
Yorick, slave COL 9

York, slave GRE 3
York, slave HOR 1
York, slave COL 10
York, slave of CHA 6
Dr. A. N. Toomer
Youmans, Thomas,
slave BEA 14
Young, Abigail SUM 10
Young, B. M.,
slave of LAU 7
Young, Doroh B.,
slave of LAU 3
Young, F. A.,
slave of AND 5
Young, George ABB 14
Young, James L.,
slave of LAU 3
Young, Jane GRE 5
Young, John W.,
Dr., slaves ofLAU 8
Young, Mary SUM 10
Young, Samuel,
slave of LAU 5
Young, Wm. AND 8
Young, W.,
slave of ABB 13
Young, William N.ABB 14
Youngblood, Char-
ley BAR 10
Youngblood, John,
slave of EDG 7
Youngblood,
Joseph EDG 14
Younge, Sarah CHR 2
Youngue, J. L.,
slave of FAI 3

Zeigler, William ORA 8
Zilpha, slave MRN 1
Zion, slave GRE 4
Zimmerman, E. C. SPA 1
Zorn, Eliza BAR 12

ADDENDA:

Smart, Major Henry,
slaves of BEA 1
Solomon, slave ORA 1
Sparks, Martha,
slave of CFD 2

www.ingramcontent.com/pod-product-compliance
Lightning Source LLC
Chambersburg PA
CBHW021839020426
42334CB00014B/698
9780893081942